CAMPAIGN • 235

WALCHEREN 1944

Storming Hitler's island fortress

RICHARD BROOKS   ILLUSTRATED BY GRAHAM TURNER

Series editor Marcus Cowper

First published in Great Britain in 2011 by Osprey Publishing,
PO Box 883, Oxford, OX1 9PL, UK
1385 Broadway, 5th Floor, New York, NY 10018, USA
Email: info@ospreypublishing.com

OSPREY is a trademark of Osprey Publishing, a division of
Bloomsbury Publishing Plc

Transferred to digital print on demand 2018

First published 2011
2nd impression 2012

Printed and bound in Great Britain

A CIP catalogue record for this book is available from the British Library.

ISBN: 978 1 84908 237 2
eBook PDF ISBN: 978 1 84908 238 9

Editorial by Ilios Publishing Ltd, Oxford, UK (www.iliospublishing.com)
Page layout by The Black Spot
Index by Mike Parkin
Maps by bounford.com
3D bird's-eye views by The Black Spot
Battlescene illustrations by Graham Turner
Typeset in Sabon and Myriad Pro
Originated by PDQ Media

www.ospreypublishing.com
To find out more about our auth   ors and books visit our website. Here
you will find extracts, author interviews, details of forthcoming events
and the option to sign-up for our newsletter.

ARTIST'S NOTE

Readers may care to note that the original paintings from which the
colour plates in this book were prepared are available for private sale.
The Publishers retain all reproduction copyright whatsoever.
All enquiries should be addressed to:

Graham Turner, PO Box 568, Aylesbury, Bucks, HP17 8EX, UK

The Publishers regret that they can enter into no correspondence upon
this matter.

ACKNOWLEDGEMENTS

The author would like to thank the following for their invaluable
assistance: John Ambler and Matthew Little of the Royal Marines
Museum; Major J. C. Beadle MBE MC; Kate Brett and Jenny Wraight of the
Naval Historical Branch; Ken Brooks; David Carson; Paul M. Crucq; David
Fletcher of the Royal Tank Regiment Museum; J. N. Houterman; Jeff
James; Roger Mountford; Dick Pool; J. Ruissen; Hans Sakkers; Colonel W.
Townend RA; Alison Wareham, Margaret Newman and Stephen
Courtenay of the Royal Naval Museum; the Reading Room staff at the
Imperial War Museum; the Zeeuwse Bibliotheek/Beeldbank, Middelburg.

AUTHOR'S NOTE

Allied military operations in Walcheren were conducted by First Canadian
Army and II Canadian Corps, which included units of many nationalities.
The terms British and Canadian, therefore, refer specifically to units of
those nationalities, and Allied to mixed activities or formations, including
the whole Allied Expeditionary Force.

The Dutch name is used throughout for the river Schelde, also known
as the Scheldt or Escaut, and Vlissingen, referred to as Flushing in older
English accounts.

'Commando' with a capital means a unit; 'commando' means a
member of such a unit. Commando units used cardinal numbers, e.g. 48
(RM) Commando, pronounced four-eight. Army units are identified in full
by ordinal numbers, e.g. 7th/9th Battalion The Royal Scots, or cardinal
numbers when abbreviated, e.g. 4 KOSB.

THE WOODLAND TRUST

Osprey Publishing supports the Woodland Trust, the UK's leading
woodland conservation charity. Between 2014 and 2018 our donations
are being spent on their Centenary Woods project in the UK.

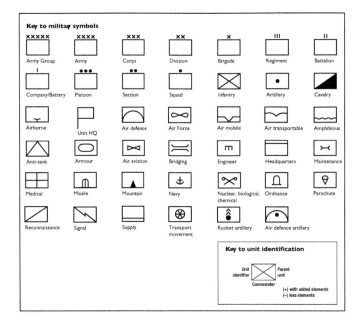

CONTENTS

The opening of the Schelde, September–November 1944

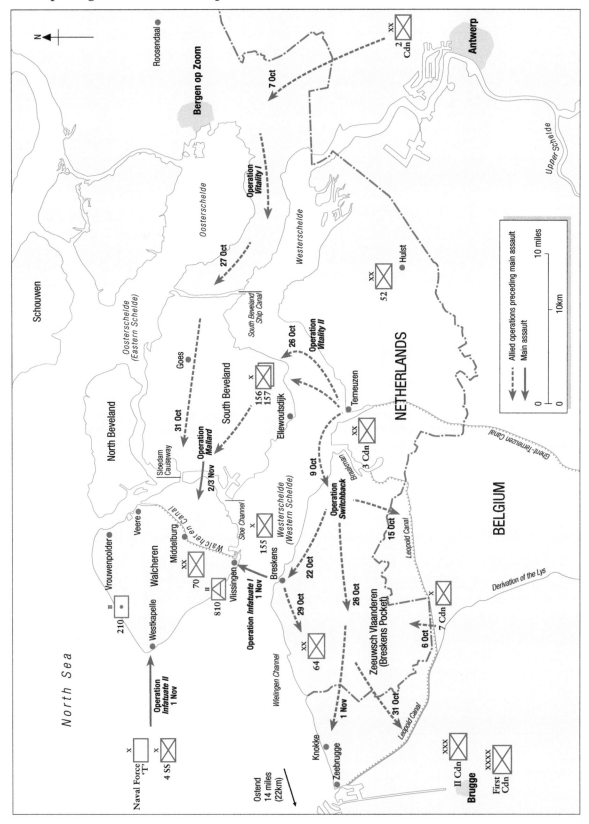

INTRODUCTION

The liberation of the Dutch island of Walcheren in November 1944, and the opening of the river Schelde, was the most significant event of the war in North-west Europe between the Normandy breakout in August of that year and the defeat of the German counteroffensive in the Ardennes the following January. It was the last great amphibious operation conducted in European waters during World War II, launched head-on against the most strongly defended stretch of coastline in the world. For the first time since the ill-starred attempt on Dieppe in 1942, a fortified harbour was assaulted, and taken. The campaign was an epic of military professionalism and raw courage, set against one of the most bizarre backdrops of the war, a sunken island surrounded by sand dunes, 30–70ft (9–21m) high, encrusted with concrete bunkers. Today it is largely forgotten, outside Walcheren itself, a dwindling band of veterans and the Royal Marines. Without it, however, the Western Allies' campaign in Europe would have faltered, and might have died.

Walcheren mattered because its coastal batteries and the minefields that they protected blocked maritime access to Antwerp, Europe's second-largest port and 70 miles (113km) from the open sea. Before the war, 11,000 sea-going ships and 44,000 river craft had entered Antwerp every year. Thanks to the Belgian Resistance, the British 11th Armoured Division captured the city intact on 4 September, with its numberless cranes and miles of wharves.

A scene from the Pacific war transferred to North-west Europe: Buffalo amphibians loaded with Marines swim ashore from an LCT off the Walcheren landing beaches, 1 November 1944. (Photo © Trustees of the Royal Marines Museum)

The ultimate objective of the assault on Walcheren: Antwerp's Kattendijk Dock packed with shipping before the war. Captured intact in September 1944, Antwerp was not open to seaborne traffic until December. (Postcard from Author's collection)

At that time, Allied land forces were still supplied over the Normandy beaches. Allied bombing or German demolition had wrecked every port from Cherbourg to Ostend. As supply lines lengthened, the Allies faced operational paralysis, unable to nourish their existing formations with ammunition and fuel, or to bring fresh American divisions into play. Three US divisions and two British sat idly in Normandy, their trucks taken away to supply the front line. Landing craft, desperately needed in the Far East, were still occupied shipping military stores across the English Channel. At any moment autumn gales might wreck the fragile Mulberry harbour at Arromanches, cutting off the flow of supplies altogether. Opening Antwerp would cut 300 miles (480km) off Allied lines of communications.

Field Marshal Sir Bernard Montgomery, whose 21st Army Group was responsible for clearing the Channel coast, was slow to take up the challenge of opening the Schelde. His own forces were better placed than the Americans to exploit what few supplies came through the Channel ports. He personally was more focused on ambitious plans for an airborne and armoured thrust across the Rhine, known as Operation *Market Garden*, to win the war by Christmas. The dangerous and less glamorous job of securing the approaches to Antwerp was left to First Canadian Army. Even after the failure of *Market Garden* on 26 September, 21st Army Group denied the Canadians priority for artillery ammunition, despite increasing pressure from General Eisenhower, the Allied Supreme Commander.

Not until mid-October, following a bruising series of high-level exchanges, did Montgomery accept the overriding need to open the Schelde to Allied shipping. On the 5th, Admiral Sir Bertram Ramsay RN, Eisenhower's naval deputy, lambasted Montgomery's uncharacteristic improvidence at a conference involving Eisenhower and Sir Alan Brooke, Chief of the Imperial General Staff, the most senior post in the British Army. On the 9th, Eisenhower forecast that all Allied operations from Switzerland to the Channel would stop unless Antwerp was operational by mid-November. Finally, Montgomery issued new directives to his army commanders on 16 October, recognizing that free use of Antwerp was vital to the Allied cause. Operations to open the port should take priority over all other offensive activity within 21st Army Group. Later Montgomery admitted he had made

The Allied command team off Normandy in June 1944: Admiral Sir Bertram Ramsey on the left, with Generals Eisenhower and Montgomery. The Walcheren campaign was Ramsey's brainchild, fostered upon an unwilling Montgomery. (Photo © Trustees of the Royal Naval Museum)

a big mistake in not paying the Schelde more attention. Had 11th Armoured Division pushed on immediately into the South Beveland Peninsula, which it had the petrol to do, Walcheren might have fallen two months sooner, with far fewer casualties.

While Montgomery drove north-east instead of north-west, large numbers of German troops who had been defending the Channel coast got away. In the weeks following the loss of Antwerp, the German Fifteenth Army ferried nine divisions back across the Schelde: a total of 90,000 men, 625 guns and 6,800 vehicles (with their horses). One division remained on the south bank around Breskens. Another occupied Walcheren itself. The others helped form a new German line north of Antwerp. This had to be rolled back before Walcheren itself could be attacked, a task which took the Canadian infantry most of October. Meanwhile, despite 21st Army Group's obstruction, the Royal Navy, the RAF and First Canadian Army had taken the first steps towards the liberation of Walcheren.

CHRONOLOGY

1944

June 6
Operation *Overlord*: Allied armies land in Normandy.

August 20
Allies break out of Normandy and pursue the Germans northwards.

September 4
British 11th Armoured Division captures Antwerp.

September 17
Operation *Market Garden*: battle of Arnhem begins.

September 23
German Fifteenth Army completes escape across river Schelde.

September 26
Operation *Market Garden*: battle of Arnhem ends.

October 3
RAF Bomber Command breaches sea dyke at Westkapelle.

5 October
Admiral Ramsay 'lambastes' Montgomery for not clearing Schelde.

6 October
Operation *Switchback*: 3rd Canadian Division assaults Leopold Canal.

7 October
RAF Bomber Command breaches sea dykes east and west of Vlissingen.

11 October
RAF Bomber Command breaches sea dyke at Veere.

16 October
Montgomery gives clearing the Schelde top priority.

22 October
Operation *Switchback*: 3rd Canadian Division takes Breskens.

24 October
Operation *Vitality*: 2nd Canadian Division attacks the South Beveland isthmus.

26 October
Operation *Vitality*: 52nd (Lowland) Division lands in South Beveland.

27 October
Operation *Infatuate*: Naval Force 'T' assembles at Ostend.

31 October	Operation *Vitality*: 2nd Canadian Division assaults Beveland–Walcheren causeway. Operation *Infatuate*: Naval Force 'T' sails from Ostend.		Operation *Mallard*: 52nd (Lowland) Division clears Beveland–Walcheren causeway. Operation *Calendar*: minesweepers reach Antwerp.
1 November	Operation *Infatuate*: British landings at Vlissingen and Westkapelle; 4th Special Service Brigade captures W13, W15 and W17 and advances to Domburg.	**5 November**	Operation *Infatuate*: 4th Special Service Brigade captures W18.
		6 November	Generalleutnant Daser surrenders to Royal Scots at Middelburg.
2 November	Operation *Infatuate*: street fighting in Vlissingen; 47 (RM) Commando assaults W11.	**7 November**	Operation *Infatuate*: 4th Special Service Brigade takes Black Hut. Operation *Mallard*: Veere surrenders.
3 November	Operation *Infatuate*: 7/9 Royal Scots capture Grand Hotel Britannia; 47 (RM) Commando captures batteries W11 and W4, links up with the Vlissingen beachhead. Operation *Mallard*: 6 Cameronians cross Sloe Channel. Operation *Calendar*: minesweepers enter Schelde.	**8 November**	Operation *Infatuate*: Vrouwenpolder surrenders. 52nd (Lowland) Division reports organized resistance on Walcheren ended.
		26 November	Operation *Calendar*: RN declares Antwerp channel open; first three coasters dock.
4 November	Operation *Infatuate*: 5 KOSB clears Vlissingen harbour; 4th Special Service Brigade resumes advance north of Domburg.	**28 November**	First convoy of 18 Liberty ships reaches Antwerp.

OPPOSING COMMANDERS

ALLIED

Allied operations in the Schelde Estuary were very much a combined affair.
General direction of the campaign was exercised jointly by **Admiral Ramsay**
and **Lieutenant-General Guy Simonds**, of the Canadian Royal Artillery.
Nominally in command of II Canadian Corps, Simonds was acting commander
of First Canadian Army, standing in for General Crerar who was absent on
sick leave. Ramsay's experience of amphibious warfare extended from
organizing the Dunkirk evacuation in 1940 through Allied invasions of Sicily
and Italy in 1943, to the Normandy landings of June 1944. Simonds had won
a reputation as an innovative if ruthless corps commander in Normandy.
Ramsay found the Canadian had an instinctive understanding of the potential
value of sea power applied to land warfare. Simonds' ability to implement
radical tactical solutions despite opposition from the less imaginative made a
decisive contribution to the Walcheren campaign's successful outcome.

General Hakewill-Smith (left) and his senior officers in discussion with Field Marshal Montgomery. World War II generals asserted their individuality with unusual headgear: Montgomery his famous double-badged Royal Tanks beret, Hakewill-Smith the glengarry of his old regiment, the Royal Scots Fusiliers. (Author's collection)

Operational details were handled for the Royal Navy by **Captain Anthony Pugsley RN**, a hard-fighting destroyer commander who would win a second bar to his DSO at Walcheren. His experience of amphibious warfare came from Normandy, where his headquarters ship was sunk beneath him. Pugsley was Ramsay's liaison officer at First Canadian Army headquarters at Bruges. Camping in the mud with the soldiers, he won their trust, and was among the first to press for an amphibious solution to the Walcheren problem.

Pugsley's military counterpart for the assault landing was **Brigadier B. W. Leicester RM**. Known as 'Jumbo', he had led the Commandos of 4th Special Service Brigade in Normandy, and had experience of planning amphibious operations as a Royal Marine staff officer. When his brigade was chosen for the Walcheren operation, Leicester moved his headquarters to Bruges, to work with Pugsley on the plans. Once landed, Leicester came under command of **Major-General Edmund Hakewill-Smith**, General Officer Commanding 52nd (Lowland) Division. Hakewill-Smith took over responsibility for land operations north of the Schelde, including Walcheren, on 30 October. A regular soldier wounded twice in World War I, he still sported his regimental glengarry as divisional commander. At some risk to his own career, he would resist pressure from II Canadian Corps to launch ill-conceived frontal assaults. Between them the Allied commanders at Walcheren formed a powerful team, combining flexibility and professional integrity with an impressive ability to work across inter-service boundaries.

GERMAN

The same was not true of the Germans. The Wehrmacht and Kriegsmarine officers defending Walcheren fought separate battles, the army focusing on the eastern approaches through South Beveland, leaving the navy to defend the seaward coastline. Wehrmacht headquarters was in Middelburg, the island's main town, 4 miles (6km) from Kriegsmarine headquarters in

Generalleutnant Wilhelm Daser, commander of 70. Infanterie-Division sitting in a British assault boat after his surrender to Major R. H. B. Johnston of 7/9 Royal Scots (on right, back to camera). Daser appeared a sick man unequal to a front-line command, but he survived until 1968. (Photo © Zeeuwse Bibliotheek/Beeldbank)

Vlissingen, the island's main harbour. Naval war diaries repeatedly attribute capture of their shore batteries to lack of infantry support. When asked to explain the poor opposition to the first British landings, **Kapitän zur See Frank Aschmann**, Seekommandant Südholland, simply replied: 'Das Heer – the Army'. Responsible for coastal batteries all around the Schelde Estuary, Aschmann's personal contribution to the Walcheren fighting was limited by his prompt departure soon after the British landed, leaving **Korvettenkapitän Otto Würdemann**, the harbour commander at Vlissingen, to be captured.

The senior Wehrmacht officer on Walcheren was **Generalleutnant Wilhelm Daser**, commander of 70. Infanterie-Division. Often depicted in a comical light, Daser was no worse than other unfortunates dug out to command one of Hitler's so-called 'fortresses'. Aged 60, with a history of heart trouble, he had been recalled from administering occupied civilians to command a static coastal division several months before the Normandy invasion. He was unlikely to inspire his troops with the energy and enthusiasm he lacked himself. **Oberst Eugen Reinhardt**, one of Daser's regimental commanders, was more dynamic. Described by Canadian interrogators as the 'self-styled king of Zealand', Reinhardt made numerous tours of inspection against the inevitable assault, until Allied air attacks and the consequent flooding confined him to Vlissingen. From then onwards, the local German commanders allowed the situation to drift, as if mesmerized by the physical difficulties of their situation.

Daser received his orders to defend Walcheren directly from General Gustav von Zangen, commander of 15. Armee. Zangen reported to Generalfeldmarschall Walter Model of Heeresgruppe B, directed since 4 September by that cynical professional Generalfeldmarschall Gerd von Rundstedt. Twice sacked and reinstated, Rundstedt possessed few illusions about his ability to influence the battle in face of the Führer's manic interference, or the Allies' material superiority. Compared with their opponents, the German commanders were a second-rate combination, unable and unwilling either to cooperate or to grip the battle.

OPPOSING FORCES

ALLIED

Admiral Ramsay ordered Pugsley to begin collecting shipping for an assault on Walcheren on 24 September, under the designation Naval Force 'T'. No naval striking force had been kept in being after Normandy, and the few ships available were past their best. Two of the Bombardment Squadron's three major units, HMS *Warspite* and *Erebus*, dated from World War I, and the former had only two of her four 15in. turrets still operational. Only 15in. guns and 500lb aircraft bombs were effective against the reinforced concrete bunkers that housed Walcheren's coastal batteries. This ruled out cruisers as bombardment vessels, and in any case sandbanks prevented such deep-draft vessels approaching the shore. The destroyers that accompanied the Bombardment Squadron were for escort purposes only.

Most of the 182 vessels involved in the Walcheren campaign would be shallow-draft landing craft. A variety of these existed, classed by the initials 'LC' followed by their function, for example LCA for Landing Craft Assault, or LCT for Landing Craft Tank. See the glossary for a full list of acronyms used below. Landing craft had flat bottoms, so they could be safely beached and extracted, unlike landing ships, which were not usually meant to be run ashore. The only landing ship at Walcheren was Pugsley's headquarters ship, HMS *Kingsmill*, a converted frigate. The most significant landing craft used at Walcheren were:

HMS *Warspite*, part of the Royal Navy's Bombardment Squadron: only the 15in. guns of a battleship or monitor had sufficient power to damage the massive German fortifications, or the range to reach them across the sandbanks of the Schelde. (Photo © Trustees of the Royal Marines Museum)

Type	Tonnage	Length	Speed	Crew	Load
LCA	10	42ft	10 knots	4–5	35 men
LCI(S)	15	105ft	12 knots	17	100 men
LCP(L)	10	37ft	20 knots	3–4	25 men
LCT(3)	350	192ft	9–10 knots	12	5 Churchill tanks
LCT(4)	200	187ft	8–9 knots	12	6 Churchill tanks

The disastrous Dieppe raid of 1942 had shown the need for well-armed support craft to accompany assaulting craft as closely as possible. Several types were developed, mostly converted from LCTs decked over to make a firing platform:

LCG(L)	Landing Craft Gun (Large) and
LCG(M)	Landing Craft Gun (Medium), both used for pillbox busting,
LCF	Landing Craft Flak for anti-aircraft cover and close-range support,
LCT(R)	Landing Craft Tank (Rocket) for suppressive area fire,
LCS(L)	Landing Craft Support (Large) developed from the LCI(S).

Armament consisted of obsolete naval guns, anti-tank and anti-aircraft guns, heavy mortars and large-calibre machine guns, depending on the intended target. The weapon mix for each type appears in the order of battle.

The LCT(R) was particularly frightening, putting down a barrage of 1,000 5in. rockets over an area 700 yards long by 150 wide (630 x 130m). They were one-shot weapons, being slow to reload after their initial outburst. The LCG(M) was not a conversion, being specially designed to slug it out with bunkers at point-blank range from the waterline. Both the LCG(M)s deployed at Walcheren were lost, suggesting a fatal flaw in the design concept.

A mixture of sailors and marines manned support craft, with the latter working the guns. The oddly named Support Squadron Eastern Flank (SSEF) were veterans of Normandy, where, after the initial landings, the support craft were concentrated east of the landing area to protect it against night attacks by human torpedoes and radio-controlled motorboats packed with high explosives. At Walcheren the SSEF would see more action and suffer more casualties in a few hours than they had in several months off Normandy.

Royal Marines also served in 4th Special Service or SS Brigade, retitled 4th Commando Brigade in December 1944, for obvious reasons. Not all commandos were marines, however. The original commandos had been volunteers from Army units. The first Royal Marine Commando unit was also formed from volunteers, in 1942. Eight more (RM) Commandos followed, numbered 41 to 48, mostly consisting of Hostilities Only conscripts. They did the same rugged training course as the volunteers, and thought themselves their equals, although 4 (Army) Commando, which joined the brigade after Normandy, probably felt differently. On 21 September, when Ramsay made it available to First Canadian Army, the brigade was investing German-held Dunkirk.

Commando organization differed from regular army practice; brigades had four units instead of three, and individual Commandos had five rifle troops of two sections, instead of four companies of three platoons. Troop establishment was 65, but 50–55 was more common at Walcheren. There was also a support troop with two Vickers machine guns and two 3in. mortars. A Commando, therefore, was much smaller than a full-strength infantry battalion, with less indirect fire capability. Royal Marine Commandos were particularly weak:

Commando	Strength on 1 Nov 1944
4 (Army)	502 (including French)
10 (Inter-Allied)	202 (HQ & two troops)
41 (RM)	420
47 (RM)	387
48 (RM)	432

Army Commandos numbered their troops, while the Royal Marines lettered theirs like warship turrets. 47 (RM) Commando, for example, had A, B, Q, X and Y, plus its Heavy Weapons Troop.

10 (Inter-Allied) Commando consisted of volunteers from occupied Europe, with French, Belgian, Dutch, Jewish and Norwegian troops. The two French troops joined 4 Commando, the few Dutch and Jews were distributed as interpreters, while the Belgian and Norwegian troops reinforced 41 (RM) Commando. These were men who had risked everything to fight against Germany. They would do so to considerable effect.

The other major ground unit committed to the assault on Walcheren was 52nd (Lowland) Division. The British Army's only mountain division, the Scottish Lowlanders soon tired of the joke that they had fought their first battle below sea level. Organization was as a standard British infantry division with three brigades of three battalions and the usual supporting services. The divisional artillery, however, included 1st Mountain Regiment with three eight-gun batteries of 3.7in. pack howitzers, besides the usual three field regiments with 25-pdrs. Some commentators thought the infantry's inexperience inclined them to take excessive risks. It might be that after five years on the war's sidelines, they felt they had something to prove.

Fortress Walcheren

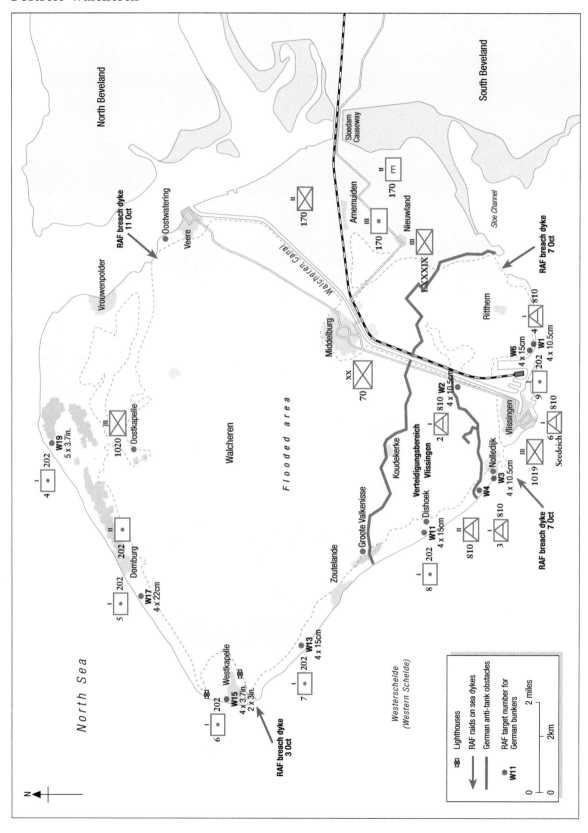

The British Army's trump card was its artillery. Over 300 guns were deployed around Breskens, surveyed in for accurate predicted fire against Walcheren's southern shores, ranging almost as far north as Domburg. Many were Canadian. Two-thirds were medium (4.5 and 5.5in.) or heavy (7.2in. and American 155mm), with half a dozen super-heavies. These were concentrated in two powerful agglomerations known as AGRA, Army Groups Royal Artillery, an organization that could bring down massive concentrations of fire with rapidity and accuracy. There was also an experimental Canadian rocket unit, known as Land Mattress, which the German commander in Vlissingen admitted was very effective.

This imposing mass of artillery had two limitations. Such relatively light calibres had no effect at all on reinforced concrete, though numerous Germans were captured in a state of incoherent shock from the continuous bombardments they had suffered. Secondly, the north-west coast, from Domburg onwards, was out of range of everything except the super-heavies and 155mm guns, which were insufficiently precise to provide close support for infantry. However, Allied progress through South Beveland brought the 52nd Division's field regiments into range from the other side, in the campaign's closing stages. The gunners may not have shared all the risks run by the infantry, but the conditions in which they laboured were equally demanding. In the Breskens Pocket, the 25-pdrs' turntables sank so far into the swampy ground that the mud reached the wheel hubs, and it took hours of backbreaking work to move the guns about.

The other invaluable asset the attackers possessed was the 79th Armoured Division, a collection of specialized armoured fighting vehicles designed to help the infantry ashore. These were used at Walcheren in two main ways:

a) As armoured assault teams intended to break down obstacles and clear minefields. There were four of these, each carried in an LCT, and made up of six waterproofed vehicles adapted for wading ashore:

One D7 armoured bulldozer.

Two Churchill Armoured Vehicles Royal Engineers (AVREs) armed with a 12in. spigot mortar for demolishing obstacles. One carried a huge bundle of sticks or 'fascine' for filling holes, the other a bridge for crossing them.

Three Sherman tanks known as Crabs or Flails, fitted with devices that whirled round detonating any mines they struck. Two teams had a Sherman command tank with the usual 75mm gun instead of one Flail.

Crews came from a mixture of armoured regiments, depending on the vehicle, as shown in the order of battle. Five more armoured bulldozers belonging to Royal Engineer Field Companies landed on the first day, and three more later on.

b) As Assault Squadrons Royal Engineers equipped with Landing Vehicles Tracked or LVT, an armoured amphibious personnel carrier. Developed from Florida swamp buggies, these were so popular with the US Marines in the Pacific they had only just become available to the British, who called them Buffaloes. There were two versions: LVT(2) and LVT(4), the latter having more freeboard and a hinged tail ramp, allowing it to carry small guns and vehicles. A normal load might be 30 infantry or four tons of cargo. Maximum speeds were 25mph on land or 7mph in water (40 and 11kmph), although the sand and minefields of Walcheren made walking pace more usual. The British mounted 20mm Polsen guns on their LVTs, making them a bit more like tanks. They were noisy and mechanically unreliable, but without them Walcheren could not have been taken.

Each Commando also received 20 'Weasels', a smaller tracked amphibian. These proved less successful in the difficult conditions around Walcheren. Many were lost in the initial landings, along with their precious stores and wireless sets.

The amphibians were launched from LCTs on or near the beach. Loads varied between three–six Buffaloes and three–seven Weasels per LCT, usually mixed depending on tactical requirements. Serial 18, for example, consisted of 47 (RM) Commando's headquarters and B Troop. It had six Buffaloes, one from 509 Field Company RE, and four Weasels. Five assault squadrons crewed the LVTs at Westkapelle, distributed one to each of the three Commandos, one to brigade headquarters, and one to medical units. Personnel came from the Royal Engineers and 11th Royal Tank Regiment. At Vlissingen, 11 RTR provided crews for another 20 LVTs and 26 Weasels, running a ferry service across the Schelde to support the 52nd Division once a bridgehead was established.

Air operations in close support (Typhoon and Spitfire fighter-bombers) were under the direction of 84 Group RAF in Belgium, with liaison to Bomber Command in the United Kingdom via 84 Group or First Canadian Army as necessary.

GERMAN

Allied intelligence estimated there were 7,000–10,000 Germans defending Walcheren, drawn from three main sources:

a) The German Navy or Kriegsmarine provided two artillery regiments, or *Abteilungen*, each about 900 strong: Marine-Artillerie-Abteilung 202 and Marine-Flak-Abteilung 810. Each had several batteries, distributed among ten strongpoints identified by RAF target numbers beginning 'W', as shown in the order of battle. Different sources quote various figures for the total guns mounted. The authoritative Naval Historical Branch study gives 44 in all. MAA 202's main armament, counting only those heavy guns capable of sinking ships, comprised the 27 listed. All these could fire on the Western Schelde and the landing beaches, except W19 at Oostkapelle. This faced northwards, towards the Eastern Schelde.

Naval personnel were a cut above the military garrison. The British attributed the enemy's protracted resistance in north-western Walcheren to the large proportion of Kriegsmarine gunners fighting as infantry. Once captured, the large, well-turned-out German sailors contrasted strangely with the undersized, scruffy infantrymen. A number of E-boats and explosive motorboats were thought to be based on Walcheren, but none of these were encountered.

b) 70. Infanterie-Division had been a standard German division with three regiments of two battalions, plus *Füsilier-* and *Pionier-Bataillone* that doubled as infantry, and an *Artillerie-Regiment* of three *Abteilungen*. By late October 1944 the division had fallen victim to the German policy of taking improvised *Kampfgruppen* away from their parent formations. The main loss was Grenadier-Regiment 1018, detached with an *Artillerie-Abteilung* to the mainland. Detachments to South Beveland caused further attrition, aggravated by the peculiar character of the parent division. 70. Infanterie-Division was a *Magenkranken-Division*, 90 per cent of its infantry suffering from chronic

stomach disorders. Nicknamed *Weissbrot*, because it ate white bread instead of the usual indigestible black, the division enjoyed a special diet of noodles, mashed potatoes and stewed fruit. By mid-October sickness and combat had reduced its remaining battalions to 350–400 men apiece, and many heavy weapons had been lost. Documents captured in Vlissingen by 4 Commando suggest Grenadier-Regiment 1019 was down to quarter strength.

Daser thought his command adequate for the defensive role it played until August, but criticized its subsequent use in mobile front-line operations. Canadian intelligence considered its members: 'hardly fitted to supply a firm backbone to the defences… may well offer adequate resistance in the early stages of an attack, even if their fundamental weakness causes them to go to pieces rapidly as they lose their officers'. The key question was how far residual fanaticism and concern about families at home exposed to Nazi reprisals, would counteract exposure to massive air and ground bombardments, interspersed with long periods confined to damp bunkers. The eagerness that many of Walcheren's garrison showed to surrender suggests that present danger outweighed more distant commitments to family and Führer.

c) Festung-Stamm-Truppen LXXXIX was a fortress regiment brought in to replace Grenadier-Regiment 1018. Sometimes described as a battalion, it had ten four-platoon companies of about 130 men, armed with French rifles and mortars, and a few anti-tank guns. Canadian intelligence described them as, 'not one of the Führer's favourite units'. Most of the men were over 40, and the rest were recycled casualties from the Eastern Front. Such troops were insufficient to compensate for the garrison's numerical or moral weakness. Even with them, there were only 20 infantry per mile of coastline. Few riflemen were encountered on the landing beaches, and none of the prisoners questioned had made any attempt to resist.

Besides these major formations, numerous other units were identified, including miscellaneous Kriegsmarine and Luftwaffe personnel, besides disorganized fragments from South Beveland and the Breskens Pocket. They increased the POW count, but added little to the garrison's powers of resistance. These depended upon the island's fixed fortifications. Declared a fortress on 4 September, Walcheren was more so than most. The Germans had constructed about 300 major bunkers on the island with walls and roofs some 7ft (2m) thick, besides hundreds of smaller works such as the Tobruk, a concrete rifle pit. Bunker designs were standardized along the whole

LEFT
Support craft preparing for the Normandy invasion in Southampton: the nearest vessel is a Landing Craft Gun (Large) with a Landing Craft Flak Mark 4 to starboard, and two more LCG(L)s beyond. (Photo © Trustees of the Royal Marines Museum)

RIGHT
German coastal defences under construction at Valkenisse in 1942. The rows of posts running out to sea are Dutch breakwaters, connected by rows of wooden stakes and steel tetrahedra, with minefields on the open beach opposite Zouteland church. (Photo © Zeeuwse Bibliotheek/Beeldbank)

Many of the German heavy guns at Walcheren were war booty: one of W15's British 3in. guns after its capture; behind it is the battery command bunker with its flat-topped observation room. (Photo © Trustees of the Royal Marines Museum)

Atlantic Wall, from Norway to the Pyrenees. Each had its own specific purpose, and was identified by a three-digit number, such as the 134K Küchenunterstand or kitchen bunker. Accommodation and munitions bunkers were typically inland, concealed on the reverse slope of the dunes, or among the trees near farm buildings. The eyes and teeth of the defence lay to seaward, with observation and command bunkers, and massive gun casemates. These were sited well forward, in accordance with Kriegsmarine doctrine, giving them good fields of fire out to sea. Wireless and telephone cable bunkers kept communications open, usually until just before the enemy came in the door.

The Walcheren fortifications consisted of two main groups: the Freie Küste or open coast to the west, running from Veere past Westkapelle and southwards, and secondly the self-contained Verteidigungsbereich Vlissingen, or Vlissingen defensive area. The latter was particularly strong, enclosed to the north by defences stretching from Groote Valkenisse through Koudekerke and Oost-Souburg to Ritthem, and back along the seafront to the south. Among the refinements were manhole covers adapted for sniper fire. Besides the heavy guns discussed above, weapons ranged from Czech 4.5cm anti-tank guns up to 10.5cm anti-aircraft guns. Many, however, including two-thirds of the 10.5cm Flak at Vlissingen, had been removed or lost before the British arrived.

Beach obstacles took various forms: multiple rows of 10ft (3m) poles, a third of them with shells on the top; steel girder tetrahedrons or 'hedgehogs'; and 'Element C', a massive steel fence that took a bulldozer to shift it. Other poles were rigged to explode artillery shells when disturbed. Conventional mines were sown around company positions and along the coast, where they sank harmlessly into the sand to be churned up later by passing vehicles. Besides French anti-tank mines, there were anti-personnel S-Minen, called Schumines by the British, and Holzminen in wooden boxes, which defied magnetic detection. More exotic accessories included land-based torpedo tubes, fixed flame-throwers, rocket projectors and remote-controlled demolition vehicles called Goliaths. The value of these elaborate physical defences, however, was undermined by the lack of decent infantry to defend them, or commanders resolute enough to make them do so.

ORDERS OF BATTLE

ALLIED FORCES

NAVAL FORCES

Naval Force 'T' – Captain A. F. Pugsley RN
NB: Shows vessels and craft used on 1 November, not all those available.

Headquarters shipping
HMS *Kingsmill* (USN Captain-class frigate 3 x 3in.)
LCH x 1, Deputy Senior Officer Assault Group (controls beaching)
LCI(L) x 3
LCI(S) x 10 (assault & rescue)
ML x 4 (navigational leaders)
LCP(L) x 12 (smoke laying)
LCP(Sy) x 2 (navigational leaders)
LCV(P) x 2 (port duties Ostend)
LCA(OC) x 3 (port duties Ostend)
Landing barges x 8 (stores, maintenance and watering at Ostend)

Bombardment Squadron – Captain M. H. A. Kelsey RN
HMS *Warspite* (Queen Elizabeth-class battleship 4 x 15in.)
HMS *Erebus* (monitor 2 x 15in.)
HMS *Roberts* (monitor 2 x 15in.)
HMS *Garth* (Hunt-class destroyer: 4 x 4in.)
HMS *Cottesmore* (Hunt-class destroyer: 4 x 4in.)
HMS *Growler* (tug)

Support Squadron Eastern Flank – Commander K. A. Sellar RN
LCH x 2 (squadron commander and deputy)
LCG(L) x 6 (2 x 4.7in.)
LCG(M) x 2 (2 x 17-pdr)
LCF x 6 (4 x 2-pdr pom-poms and 8 x 20mm Oerlikons)
LCS(L) x 6 (6-pdr anti-tank gun; 2 x 20mm Oerlikons; twin .5in. Vickers; 4in. smoke mortar)
LCT(R) x 5 (1,080 x 5in. rocket launchers)

'H' LCA Squadron – Lieutenant-Commander S. J. Vernon RN (Breskens)
LCA x 72 (6 flotillas of 12+)

'N' LCT Squadron – Lieutenant-Commander B. K. C. Arbuthnot RN (Ostend)
LCT(3) x 6 (4 Flotilla)
LCT(4) x 30 (20, 22 and 47 Flotillas)

Attached:
A Troop No. 3 Combined Operations Bombardment Unit (6 x forward observer bombardment or FOB)
A & B LCOCU (Landing Craft Obstacle Clearance Units)
RN Beach Commando 'L'
No. 2 Beach Signals Section RN

Minesweeping flotillas (Operation *Calendar*)
Minesweeping Force 'A' (river clearance) – Captain H. G. Hopper RN, Sheerness
    HMS *Tudno* (headquarters ship) plus motor launch (ML) as tender
    157th, 159th, 165th Flotillas: British Yard
    minesweepers (BYMS) with Oropesa and magnetic sweeps x3 0
    102nd, 110th, 131st, 139th, 140th Flotillas: motor minesweepers (MMS) with
    magnetic sweeps x 36
    15th, 19th Flotillas: MLs with Oropesa sweeps x 16
    197th, 198th, 199th Flotillas: motor fishing vessels (MFV) with magnetic sweeps
    x 24
    704th Flotilla: LCP(L)s with snag-line sweeps x 6
    Trawlers for stores, fuelling and survey x 7
    MFV for sweep maintenance x 1
Total 122 ships and craft

Minesweeping Force 'B' (estuary clearance) – Captain T. W. Marsh RN, Harwich
    Fleet sweepers and MMS as required, including:
    160th Flotilla (BYMS)
    Belgian manned MMS x 5
Total 50 ships at peak

LAND FORCES

British battalions had four rifle companies of about 120 men each; Commandos had five rifle and one support troops of 50–60 men. Field artillery regiments had three eight-gun batteries of 25-pdr gun-howitzers; medium or heavier regiments had four four-gun batteries of 4.5in. guns or upwards.

52nd (Lowland) Division – Major-General Edmund Hakewill-Smith:

Infatuate I
155th (Lowland) Infantry Brigade – Brigadier J. F. S. McLaren
    7th/9th (Highlanders) Battalion The Royal Scots – Lieutenant-Colonel
     M. E. Melvill
    4th (The Border) Battalion The King's Own Scottish Borderers (4 KOSB) –
    Lieutenant-Colonel C. L. Melville
    5th (Dumfries & Galloway) Battalion The King's Own Scottish Borderers (5 KOSB)
    – Lieutenant-Colonel W. F. R. Turner
    Platoon A Company and C Company 7th Battalion The Manchester Regiment
    (4.2in. mortars and Vickers machine guns)
    452 Battery, 1st Mountain Regiment (8 x 3.7in. pack howitzers)
    241 Field Company Royal Engineers

Under command:
4 (Army) Commando – Lieutenant-Colonel R. W. P. Dawson
10 (Inter-Allied) Commando – Commandant P. Kieffer (No. 1 & 8 French Troops:
renumbered 5 & 6 within 4 Cdo)
A Squadron 11th Royal Tank Regiment (20 x LVTs, 26 x Weasels)
Platoon 59 GHQ Troops Royal Engineers
6th Field Dressing Station RCAMC
Section 144th Company Pioneer Corps

Infatuate II
4th Special Service Brigade – Brigadier B. W. Leicester RM
    41 (Royal Marine) Commando – Lieutenant-Colonel E. C. E. Palmer RM
    47 (Royal Marine) Commando – Lieutenant-Colonel C. Farndale Phillips RM
    48 (Royal Marine) Commando – Lieutenant-Colonel J. L. Moulton RM
    No. 10 (Inter-Allied) Commando – Lieutenant-Colonel P. Laycock (No. 2 Dutch,
    No. 4 Belgian & No. 5 Norwegian Troops)
NB: At the time 4 Commando Brigade was still known by the title shown above.

Under command:
59th GHQ Troops Royal Engineers
509 and 510 Field Company and 511 Field Park Company Royal Engineers
5th Field Transfusion Unit RCAMC
8th and 9th Field Surgical Units RCAMC
10th Field Dressing Station RCAMC
17th Light Field Ambulance RCAMC
144th Company Pioneer Corps (less 1 section)

In support of the whole operation:
79th Armoured Division – Major-General Sir Percy Hobart
30th Armoured Brigade – Brigadier N. W. Duncan
    Armoured Assault Team – Major D. R. R. Pocock
        A Squadron 1st Lothian & Border Yeomanry (Flails) – from 30th
        Armoured Brigade
        87 Squadron 6th Assault Regiment RE (AVRE) – from 1st Assault
        Brigade RE
        149th Assault Park Squadron RE (armoured bulldozers)
    LVT Regiment
        5th Assault Regiment RE – from 1st Assault Brigade RE
        Detachments 11th Royal Tank Regiment – from 33rd Armoured
        Brigade

Artillery at Breskens (total 314 guns):
2nd Canadian Divisional Artillery (less 5th Regiment RCA in South Beveland)
    4th and 6th Regiments RCA (48 x 25-pdr)
    61st and 110th Regiments RA (48 x 25-pdr)
2nd Army Group Royal Canadian Artillery:
    3rd and 4th Medium Regiments RCA (16 x 4.5in.; 16 x 5.5in.)
    15th Medium Regiment RA (16 x 5.5in.)
    1st Heavy Regiment RA (less two 155mm batteries) (8 x 7.2in.)
    52nd Heavy Regiment RA (8 x 7.2in.; 8 x 155mm)

3rd Super Heavy Regiment RA (4 x 240mm; 2 x 8in.)
9th Army Group Royal Artillery:
    9th, 10th, 11th, and 107th Medium Regiments RA (64 x 5.5in.)
    51st Heavy Regiment RA (8 x 7.2in.; 8 x 155mm)
    59th (Newfoundland) Heavy Regiment RA (less one 155mm battery)
    (8 x 7.2in.; 4 x 155mm)
76th Anti-Aircraft Brigade (in ground role):
    112nd and 113th Heavy AA Regiments RA (24 x 3.7in.)

Operating in South Beveland and north-east Walcheren
5th Canadian Infantry Brigade – Brigadier W. J. Megill
    The Black Watch of Canada – Lieutenant-Colonel B. R. Ritchie
    The Calgary Highlanders – Major R. L. Ellis
    Le Regiment de Maisonneuve – Lieutenant-Colonel J. Bibeau
    7th Field Company Royal Canadian Engineers
156th (Lowland) Infantry Brigade – Brigadier C. N. Barclay
    4th/5th Battalion The Royal Scots Fusiliers – Lieutenant-Colonel A. N. Gosselin
    6th (Lanarkshire) Battalion The Cameronians (Scottish Rifles) – Lieutenant-
    Colonel A. I. Buchanan-Dunlop
    7th Battalion The Cameronians (Scottish Rifles) – Lieutenant-Colonel C. F. Nason
157th (Lowland) Infantry Brigade – Brigadier J. D. Russell
    5th Battalion The Highland Light Infantry – Lieutenant-Colonel R. L. C. Rose
    6th Battalion The Highland Light Infantry – Lieutenant-Colonel E. L. Percival
    1st Battalion Glasgow Highlanders The Highland Light Infantry – Lieutenant-
    Colonel W. I. French
52nd Divisional Artillery:
    79th (Lowland) Field Regiment RA (24 x 25-pdr)
    80th (Lowland) Field Regiment RA (24 x 25-pdr)
    186th Field Regiment RA (24 x 25-pdr)
    1st Mountain Regiment RA (24 x 3.7in. pack howitzers – less 8 guns in
    Vlissingen)
52nd Divisional Engineers:
    202 Field Company RE
    554 Field Company RE
    243 Field Park Company RE

AIR FORCES

RAF Bomber Command – preliminary bombardments
84 Group 2nd Tactical Air Force (RAF) – all resources available throughout the
operation:
    Typhoon squadrons   x 10
    Spitfire squadrons   x 15
    Mustang squadrons   x 1
11 Group RAF – air spotting for naval bombardment:
    Nos. 26 and 63 Squadrons (Hurricane and Spitfire)
Air Observation Post – spotting for naval and artillery bombardments:
    Nos. 660 and 661 Squadrons (Auster)

GERMAN FORCES

WEHRMACHT

70. Infanterie-Division (Middelburg) – previously 165. Reserve-Division –
Generalleutnant Wilhelm J. Daser (Festungskommandant Walcheren)
    Grenadier-Regiment 1019 (Vlissingen; south-west Walcheren) – Oberst E. J.
    Reinhardt (Kommandant Verteidigungsbereich Vlissingen)
        I. Bataillon (Vlissingen) – Hauptmann Rode
        II. Bataillon (south-east Walcheren; Fort Rammekens) – Hauptmann
        W. Heine
    Grenadier-Regiment 1020 (Oostkapelle; north-west Walcheren) –
    Oberstleutnant W. Veigele
        I. Bataillon – Major Müller
        II. Bataillon – Hauptmann Schicke
    Artillerie-Regiment 170 (Middelburg; batteries at Arnemuiden and Nieuwland) –
    Oberst F. Lex
    Divisions-Füsilier-Bataillon 170 (north-east Walcheren; Sloe Channel–Veere) –
    Major G. Maier
    Pionier-Bataillon 170 (Sloe Channel) – Hauptmann K. Winter
    Festung-Stamm-Truppen LXXXIX (Nieuwland; east Walcheren) Oberst O. Gajer:
    originally three battalions, reduced to one by detachments

KRIEGSMARINE

Seekommandant Südholland (Vlissingen) –
Kapitän zur See F. Aschmann
Marine-Artillerie-Abteilung 202 (Domburg) –
Korvettenkapitän R. Opalka
    Gefechtstand (headquarters) (1/202)
    Marineküstenbatterie Oostkapelle (4/202) W19, 5 x 3.7in. (British AA guns)
    Marineküstenbatterie Domburg (5/202) W17, 4 x 22cm and 1 x 5cm
    Marineküstenbatterie Westkapelle (6/202) W15, 4 x 3.7in. (British AA guns),
    2 x 3in. (British AA guns)
    Marineküstenbatterie Zoutelande (7/202) W13, 4 x 15cm, 2 x 7.5cm, 3 x 2cm Flak
    Vierling
    Marineküstenbatterie Dishoek (8/202) W11, 4 x 15cm
    Marineküstenbatterie Kernwerk (9/202) W6, 4 x 15cm
    Leichte Flakbatterie
Marine Flak Abteilung 810 (north-west Vlissingen) – Korvettenkapitän H. Köll
    Gefechtstand (headquarters) (1/810) W4
    Marineflakbatterie Nord (2/810) W2
    Marineflakbatterie West (3/810) W3
    Marineflakbatterie Ost (4/810) W1
    Leichte Flakbatterie Seedeich (6/810)
Hafenkommandant Vlissingen – Korvettenkapitän O. Würdemann

4 Commando's monument in Vlissingen's Commandoweg, once the site of Uncle Beach. In the background, the Oranjemolen where the British first landed. The multi-lingual inscription reads: 'To the memory of the officers, NCOs and men of 4 Commando and the loyal citizens of Vlissingen'. (Photo © Richard Brooks)

OPPOSING PLANS

WALCHEREN AND THE SCHELDE

The physical configuration of the Schelde Estuary severely constrained Allied and German strategic options. Walcheren, in common with the south bank of the Schelde, was man-made polderland, reclaimed from the sea over many years, often below sea level. Fighting in such terrain presented unusual difficulties to both sides.

Walcheren was originally the westernmost of several islands lying between the Ooster- and the Westerschelde (East and West Schelde). It dominated the estuary much as the Isle of Wight commands access to Southampton Water, or the Isle of Arran to the Clyde. Despite their names, the Schelde's two branches lie north and south of the South Beveland isthmus, which joins Walcheren to the mainland north of Antwerp. The only watery connections between East and West Schelde were ship canals, and the Sloe Channel between Walcheren and South Beveland. The only way across the latter was a narrow causeway, dead straight and completely open.

Walcheren is often described as a saucer, or a soup plate with a chipped rim consisting of high dunes of loose soft sand. Infantry might scramble up these, but not vehicles. Dykes filled the gaps in the dunes, keeping the sea out of the rich farmland within. The Westkapelle dyke was particularly impressive, 3 miles long (5km), 200–250ft thick at the base rising 30ft above the shore (70–80m and 10m). Constructed in the Middle Ages, it was considered the oldest, finest and most solid dyke in the Netherlands.

The branch of the Schelde that mattered in late 1944 was the Westerschelde, Walcheren's southern moat and the seaway to Antwerp. On its southern bank, roughly opposite Vlissingen, lay the fishing port of Breskens. Further south, the Leopold Canal curved round from Zeebrugge on the Channel coast to the Schelde forming an ideal defensive redoubt 25 miles wide and 20 deep (40 x 32km). This had to be cleared first to provide a staging post for an Allied amphibious assault across the estuary, and also to silence German batteries between Breskens and Knokke.

ALLIED

Compared with the lengthy preparations for the Normandy landings, planning for Walcheren was compressed into a few weeks. It evolved rapidly under the pressure of events, as the military situation unfolded. The planners at First Canadian Army had originally rejected a full-blown assault landing as taking too long to prepare. They hoped instead to seize bridgeheads with airborne troops, who could be reinforced using LCAs and amphibians. First Airborne Army declined the mission, however, dismissing Walcheren as an unsuitable drop zone.

Pugsley's arrival at First Canadian Army on 20 September coincided with Simonds drafting a memo that stated, 'an assault across water cannot be ruled out if Walcheren must be taken'. Next day, as Pugsley began to assemble a naval planning staff, Ramsay released 4th Special Service Brigade as the basis of a landing force. Unit commanders received final plans for the assault just over a month later on 24 October. By then the Walcheren landings had become the final stage of a three-phase programme, two of which were already well under way.

First of all, 3rd Canadian Division began Operation *Switchback* to clear the Breskens Pocket. The Germans, however, flooded the low-lying countryside to create conditions of 'ground saturation'. This preserved the farms for their own use, while confining the attackers to well-defined lines of attack along the raised roads. Exposed to fire and unable to manoeuvre, the Canadians advanced slowly and painfully. In the last week of October, 2nd Canadian Division began an equally difficult offensive in South Beveland, cutting Walcheren off from the mainland.

Simonds had predicted the Germans' partial flooding of the battlefield, and suggested an appropriate countermeasure. RAF Bomber Command

Composite aerial view of the coast south of Westkapelle as used to plan the landings – the corners of the prints still show the pinholes that held them together. The large square structure on the left is the Giant Würzburg radar station, its circular antenna side-on to the camera. (Photo © Trustees of the Royal Marines Museum)

should breach the dykes, and completely flood all parts of Walcheren below high water level. This would submerge German artillery positions outside the dunes, and isolate their infantry units, making it impossible for them to launch their customary counterattacks. As a bonus, the bombing would create new beaches, not covered by existing defences, and allow the attackers to sail through the gaps in the dyke to attack the German batteries from the rear. Bomber Command was sceptical, but Simonds persuaded them by stressing the heavy casualties that would otherwise occur. Precise aiming points were specified, carefully calculated using stereoscopic aerial photographs and tide projections. On 1 October, Supreme Headquarters Allied Expeditionary Force (SHAEF) approved the drowning of Walcheren.

Simonds hoped that concentrated bombing of the remaining dry parts of the island would persuade the defenders to surrender. In case it did not, Pugsley and Leicester planned an amphibious assault in two parts:

Hand-drawn *Panzerzielskizze* or 'armoured target sketch': a visual aid for German anti-tank gunners showing the ammunition to be used at different ranges, against different targets, and the best aiming points. (Photo © Trustees of the Royal Marines Museum)

Infatuate I: 155th (Lowland) Brigade, led by 4 Commando, would assault Vlissingen under cover of darkness. Once the commandos had gained a bridgehead, the infantry would pass through to clear the town and exploit north to Middelburg, linking up with 156th Brigade advancing from South Beveland.

Infatuate II: 4th Special Service Brigade, less 4 Commando but including most of the armour, would secure a bridgehead at Westkapelle with the primary intention of advancing south-east along the dunes towards Vlissingen to silence the batteries covering the Westerschelde. They would then turn round, and clear the north-west coast as far as Vrouwenpolder.

H-hour would be 0545hrs at Vlissingen and 0945hrs at Westkapelle. This ensured a degree of surprise for *Infatuate I*, whose leading waves might hope to escape German artillery fire until they had landed. *Infatuate II*, however, needed daylight for the great mass of shipping and vehicles involved, and a rising tide to lift off any craft that ran aground during the approach. Once ashore, the soldiers needed five hours of daylight to consolidate the bridgehead. The right combination of tide and daylight occurred on 1 November. Uncertainty remained until the last minute, however. Bad weather might delay the landing at Westkapelle, or 4 Commando might not find a suitable beach at Vlissingen. In that case 155th Brigade would have to land at Westkapelle.

155th Brigade and 4 Commando were to cross the Schelde in LCAs. These were insufficiently seaworthy to use off Walcheren's exposed western coast, but small enough to transport by ship, railway and canal from England to Terneuzen on the Schelde. From there they could sail down to Breskens. The rest of 4th Special Service Brigade would sail from Ostend. Most of the Royal Marine Commandos would land in amphibians launched from LCTs, before or after the latter had beached, hopefully ensuring that tactical units landed together with their weapons and stores intact. Unlike Normandy there was no massive follow-up. The job had to be done with the forces put ashore on D-day.

Long-range naval gunfire support would come from the Bombardment Squadron, directed by specially trained observers in fighter aircraft. These, however, were based in southern England, at the mercy of autumnal mists. The support craft were closer to hand, but their weapons were far too light to make any lasting impression on Walcheren's concrete bunkers. It had been observed in Normandy, however, that German gunners invariably fired back at anyone firing on them. The SSEF might, therefore, distract the defending gunners long enough for the commandos to get ashore and attack them from behind.

A final heavy bombing raid against the Vlissingen dock area was scheduled for shortly before H-hour, with additional artillery fire in case this had to be cancelled because of bad weather. *Infatuate I* was independent of immediate air support. Once safely established ashore the troops would call for support through the Air Support Signals Unit (ASSU) channels that were commonplace in 21st Army Group. Typhoon and Spitfire fighter-bombers from 84 Group would support *Infatuate II* from H-hour onwards, subject to the weather.

Four field regiments and two medium regiments provided a basic artillery fire plan from H-15 minutes to H+90. Another medium regiment stood by to answer calls for fire from 4 Commando, while four more were available for counterbattery tasks. The heavy and super-heavy guns would engage additional targets in lieu of heavy bombing. All guns were available on call against a large number of pre-selected targets, after completion of the basic fire plan.

GERMAN

Allied fluidity contrasts with the rigidity of the defenders' plans. These were literally set in concrete, leaving no possibility of manoeuvre or retreat. When the invasion came, Rundstedt entertained no false hopes of influencing the struggle for Walcheren. Inaccessible by sea or land, 'the length of the fighting there depends entirely on the steadfastness of the garrison which cannot possibly receive support from the outside'. General Zangen made this clear on 7 October, ordering every man in the Schelde fortresses to hold out to the bitter end. They simply had to gain time, while fresh divisions built up Fortress Europe's inner lines of resistance: 'The German people are watching us. In this hour, the fortifications along the Schelde estuary occupy a role which is decisive for the future of our people. Each additional day that you deny the port of Antwerp to the enemy and to the resources that he has at his disposal will be vital.'

German refusal to give ground played into Allied hands. Daser reacted to the Canadian advance through South Beveland by fragmenting his division, instead of concentrating around the crucial batteries. Contesting ground of no value, he exhausted his fragile units, before pulling them back to the last-ditch locations shown in the order of battle. While the Kriegsmarine held the high dunes along the western coast, Daser focused exclusively on Walcheren's eastern defences. When the onslaught came, he failed to make any coherent response, supinely awaiting the Allied blows.

THE WALCHEREN CAMPAIGN

SHAPING THE BATTLEFIELD

Preparatory operations essential for the assault on Walcheren went on side by side with detailed planning of the landings themselves. While landing craft were assembled, commandos and tank crews trained, and reconnaissance parties probed the defences, the RAF and Canadians set the stage for the final assault.

The most dramatic event was Bomber Command's remodelling of the island's landscape. Using 1,000lb and 4,000lb bombs, Lancaster heavy bombers led by Mosquito pathfinders blasted four separate gaps in Walcheren's sea defences:

Date	Location	Aircraft	Bombs dropped
3 October	Westkapelle	247 Lancasters	1,274 tons
7 October	Nolledijk (north-west of Vlissingen)	58 Lancasters	348 tons
7 October	Ritthem (east of Vlissingen)	63 Lancasters	384 tons
11 October	Oostwatering (north-west of Veere)	60 Lancasters	374 tons

The crews attacked in daylight, and achieved great accuracy, the Vlissingen dykes rolling into the sea 'like rotten bread'. One Lancaster flew so low, it returned with telephone wire wrapped round it. Within days Vlissingen's lower parts were under 3ft (1m) of water. In some areas the floods rose to 10 or 11 feet (3m). The population took refuge upstairs, or moved to higher ground around Middelburg. Civilian casualties were lower than might have been expected, despite people ignoring the leaflets, dropped on 2 October, telling them to leave: 198 were killed, more by bombing than drowning. The worst incident was at Westkapelle where 47 people died sheltering in the basement of a windmill beside the dyke.

Militarily the bombardment fully justified Simonds' expectations. Tidal action soon widened the Westkapelle gap from its original 75–100 yards (70–90m) to 385 yards (350m), the sea water rushing through at eight knots (14kmph). German attempts to build a secondary dyke inland with forced labour were a hopeless failure. Soon the floods divided the island into three parts: the coastal dunes, Vlissingen and the high ground to the east, connected only by the road embankments between them. German reserves were immobilized, and most of their field batteries submerged. One disappointment was the German success in patching up their communications, which continued in operation to the end. The inundation changed a conventional land warfare problem into one of destroying a line of coastal batteries on a narrow strip of land. Protected only by their local defences, and with limited capacity for mutual support, these could now be picked off, one at a time.

Attempts to soften up the island's military defences by aerial bombardment were less successful. Too many targets were attacked with too little thought about which ones really mattered, or how many bombs were needed to achieve the desired result. A three-day bomber offensive at the end of October dropped 3,271 tons of bombs on various targets, but out of 649 sorties only 167 targeted coastal batteries. Of these just 95 went for W11, W13 or W15, whose guns directly threatened the landing beaches. Further attacks on the night of 31 October were cancelled because of bad weather. So too was the heavy bombing raid planned on Vlissingen an hour before H-hour (H-60, i.e. 0445hrs). Had the air attacks concentrated exclusively on the relevant batteries, there would have been a far higher chance of scoring the direct hits needed to take out a concrete gun emplacement. A subsequent report by 21st Army Group's operational research group (AORG Report No. 299) suggested that three-quarters of the guns nearest Westkapelle could have been destroyed had the bombing focused exclusively on W13 and W15. As it was, nearly all the main guns in W11, W13 and W15 were in action on D-day. German prisoners admitted the heavy bombing shook them up, but the delay between the raids and landings gave them time to recover. In the same period, RAF fighter-bombers made 646 sorties, mostly on the Vlissingen area.

Meanwhile, II Canadian Corps overran Walcheren's outlying defences in the Breskens Pocket and South Beveland. A brigade of 3rd Canadian Infantry Division crossed the Leopold Canal on 6 October, following a flame barrage from Wasp carriers. German machine-gun fire and counterattacks pinned them to the far bank until a second brigade landed from LVTs behind the German left flank to open up the front three days later. German resistance was ferocious, and the ground so waterlogged that scouts rowed ahead of

Sea water pours through the gap that Bomber Command had blasted through Westkapelle dyke. The concentration of bomb craters on either side shows the remarkable accuracy the Lancasters achieved. (Photo © Trustees of the Royal Marines Museum)

supply lorries in boats. Reinforced by 52nd (Lowland) Division, the Canadians took Breskens on 22 October, allowing RN bomb-disposal teams to begin clearing the harbour. By 2 November, German naval situation reports described the Cadzand battery as, 'im Endkampf stehen', making its last stand. Resistance south of the Schelde ended the next day, with the surrender of 12,707 Germans. Total losses for 3rd Canadian Infantry Division had been 2,077, including 314 dead.

2nd Canadian Infantry Division fought their way onto South Beveland on 23 October, isolating Walcheren from the mainland. Progress westwards was then quite rapid, the Canadians forcing the South Beveland ship canal, a truly major obstacle, on the 29th. Next day they linked up with 157th Brigade of 52nd (Lowland) Division who had landed behind German lines at Ellewoutsdijke, using a mixture of LCAs, LVTs and amphibious tanks. Once again, the Allies demonstrated their ability to outflank seemingly impassable positions with imaginatively handled amphibious forces. October ended with Allied forces closing up on the eastern end of the causeway leading across the Sloe Channel. The South Beveland offensive can be criticized as unnecessarily expending lives to gain territory of little value. Its main strategic effect was to force the Germans to concentrate their limited resources in Walcheren, the strategic crux of the Schelde operations, instead of dissipating them uselessly in South Beveland. On the other hand, the Allied presence east of the causeway opened up a third avenue of attack, and distracted 70. Infanterie-Division from the campaign's decisive point in the west.

While the Canadian infantry endured the horrors of polder fighting, the amphibious forces for *Infatuate I* and *II* were coming together. Force 'T', less the Bombardment Squadron and minesweepers, assembled at Ostend on 27 October. Many of the landing craft had been unfit for operations, requiring much attention from the maintenance staff at HMS *Squid*, the landing craft base in Southampton. Establishment of an advanced base at Ostend entailed berthing about 100 craft, accommodating over 400 officers and men, landing a mass of stores and installing the necessary wireless communications, all within the three days before D-day. Four more LCA flotillas had joined those already inside the Schelde Estuary, bringing total craft available to 72 LCAs and a number of LCPs. On 31 October the LVTs for *Infatuate I* joined them at Breskens, provoking accurate but ineffective artillery fire from across the river.

4th Special Service Brigade concentrated at de Haan, a seaside resort near Ostend. Here they built up their fitness over sand dunes similar to those on Walcheren, developed drills for assaulting German bunkers, and practised

Some of the 13,000 German POWs taken by the 3rd Canadian Division in the Breskens Pocket. The state of the road suggests the filthy conditions in which the Canadians had to fight. (Author's collection)

them against abandoned examples nearby. The general idea was to follow the crest of the dunes, working through enemy communication trenches. Assault groups followed supporting mortar fire closely, trusting to the sand's deadening effect for safety. Despite the pressure of time, officers from the SSEF came over from England to witness a demonstration, learning how best to support the ground troops. Destined for Vlissingen, 4 Commando studied aerial photographs, climbed sea walls, and practised street fighting in the ruins of Ostend. Neither time nor landing craft were available for a full-scale rehearsal, but troop- and Commando-level exercises were carried out, including liaison with tanks. Live firing was sufficiently realistic for four marines to be killed by their own PIAT, a type of spring-launched anti-tank weapon. The Lowlanders, however, had no time for practice. They arrived in Belgium in late October, and went straight into action. Their success would be a tribute to the quality of the training they had already received on the mountains and beaches of Scotland.

Normandy's beaches had been subjected to painstaking reconnaissance. At Walcheren, there was less time, the beaches were more closely guarded, and there was not much choice about where to land. Good zero feet air photographs of the coastline were scarce. Pugsley claimed they were taken by a box Brownie camera on a dark, foggy night. Nevertheless, the Canadian Air Survey produced ranges of 1/5,000- and 1/25,000-scale maps of the island, showing the defences in remarkable detail.

Physical reconnaissance of the Westkapelle gap was attempted by 4th Special Service Brigade's reconnaissance section, known as Keepforce after its commanding officer. Several attempts, codenamed *Tarbrush*, were made by night to probe the gap's turbulent waters between 15 and 27 October. The technique was to float a party quietly towards the beach in a rubber dinghy attached by rope to an 18ft (5m) dory 100 yards (90m) offshore, the whole team being transported to the scene by a motor torpedo boat. On each occasion the enemy opened up with flares, searchlights, and small-arms fire, forcing the party to withdraw before learning anything useful. 79th Armoured Division's assault teams would land on a beach of unknown composition, with calamitous results.

At Vlissingen, close reconnaissance of a seafront bristling with enemy machine-gun posts was clearly impossible. It was not even certain that the beach selected would prove practical. On D-day a *Tarbrush* party preceded 4 Commando to verify its accessibility, and contingency arrangements were in place to switch 155th Brigade to Westkapelle.

INFATUATE I: THE LANDING AT VLISSINGEN

The first British troops to land on Walcheren did so on the fortified seafront at Vlissingen. Less heavily defended beaches outside the town and east of the harbour were rejected, the ground being flooded and the wrong side of the Vlissingen–Middelburg Canal. Captain H. P. G. J. van Nahuijs, a Dutch police inspector recently escaped from Vlissingen, suggested a site south-east of the town centre, near the Oranjedijk mill, in the Ooster of Dokhaven, meaning the Eastern or Dock harbour. This was 110 yards wide and 250 deep (100 x 220m), with a rubbish dump at the inland end likely to provide firm going for vehicles. Either side of this 'beach', codenamed 'Uncle', were massive 10ft-high (3m) groynes, while defensive obstacles included rows of stakes and steel rails set in concrete. Beyond Uncle Beach, various stretches of water defined a natural bridgehead for the invaders to hold while gathering strength. To the north lay the Binnenhaven or inner harbour, and the Schelde Shipyard's dock, called Het Dok in Dutch, i.e. 'The Dock'. To the west were Vissershaven and Koopmanshaven, the Fishermen's and Merchants' docks, sometimes called the Western Harbour; beyond them lay the Spuikom, a reed-covered lake.

Very early on 1 November, the assault troops with their naval beach parties moved down to Breskens Harbour. Drizzling rain prevented the heavy bombing planned for Vlissingen waterfront, but twin-engined Mosquitoes stood in, with 20mm cannon and 500lb bombs. The narrow entrance to Uncle Beach combined with residual doubts about its suitability to inspire caution. A small reconnaissance party went first, followed by successively larger echelons of supporting troops. Planned touchdowns were as follows:

Time planned	Landing craft	Troops
0545hrs	2 LCPs, 1 LCA	*Tarbrush* and ½ troop 4 Commando
0545–0555hrs	5 LCAs	HQ + 1½ troops 4 Commando, RN beach party
0635hrs	8 LCAs	Troops 3–6 of 4 Commando
0725hrs	26 LCAs	4 KOSB in five waves
0805hrs	Allocation unknown	7 Manchesters (machine guns and 4.2in. mortars); Royal Engineers; 452 Mountain Battery

An hour before touchdown, 284 guns opened up on targets along the whole seafront from Nolle Point, just east of the gap in the dyke, along the boulevard, past Admiral de Ruyter's statue by the Merchants' Dock, to the harbour. There was no retaliation. Generalleutnant Daser claimed later that, between the flooding, the bombing and the barrage, there had been no German guns left in action in Vlissingen. For an hour, landing craft cruised the Schelde, their complements watching the fires kindled by the bombardment, the Oranjemolen's silhouette against the flames an unmistakable guide to the landing point.

The guns lifted to the flanks as the reconnaissance detachment closed the beach. The *Tarbrush* LCPs were holed by stakes, but 4 Commando's LCAs landed safely on the tip of the promontory. Its complement rushed the nearby observation bunker without firing a shot, and cut through the wire to take a 75mm gun in a pillbox. A 20mm cannon opened up from the Merchants' Dock area as the covering party came in, but fired too high. The troops passed through the gapped wire, to assault another gun emplacement, using the 5cm anti-tank gun within to support further progress along the waterfront. Lieutenant-Colonel Dawson set up Commando headquarters by the windmill, and called in his main body. By H+45 minutes when they arrived, the enemy was active with machine guns and 20mm cannon, hitting several LCAs without seriously impeding disembarkation. The risky decision to attack before first light had paid off. Casualties had been negligible, the enemy reaction confused and ineffectual.

The commandos' subsequent advance was designed to make best use of this limited period of surprise, seizing as much ground as possible before the defenders could react. The follow-up battalion from 155th Brigade would then mop up any Germans bypassed by the commandos' rapid advance, and thicken up the fighting line wherever required. This policy was highly successful, thanks to careful briefing of individuals from specially prepared maps and aerial photographs. The commandos unhesitatingly bypassed opposition to reach key objectives, leaving pockets of resistance to be dealt with later. Much of the old town remained dry, although below sea level. A resourceful Dutch engineer had blocked the main drain underneath Betje Wolffplein, keeping out the floods, and speeding the commandos' advance.

LCAs cross the Schelde on 1 November as smoke rises from Vlissingen. Besides the sailor and commando on the left, the group in the bow includes two American journalists who covered the assault. (Photo © Trustees of the Royal Marines Museum)

Infatuate I: assault landing at Vlissingen, 1 November

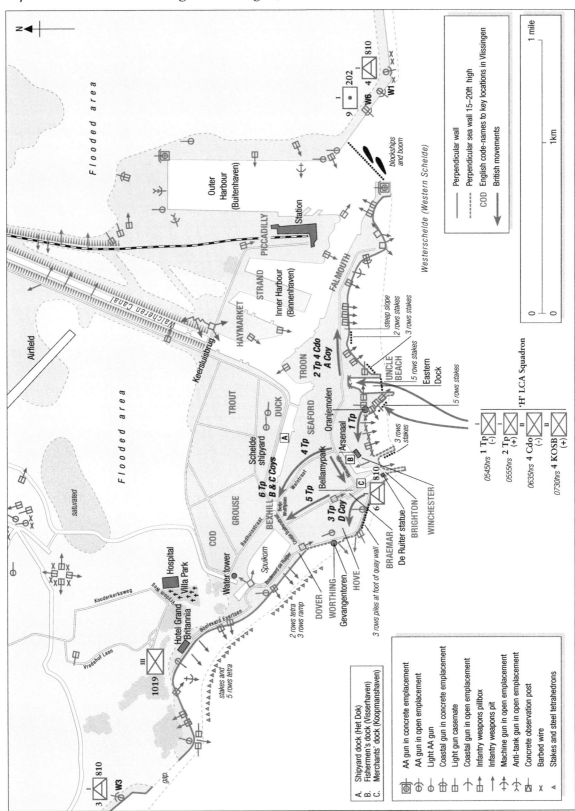

The Vlissingen battle of 1 November had two main stages: 4 Commando's expansion of the bridgehead, and its consolidation by 4 KOSB. Within these, detailed chronology is confused. The fighting is best summarized by describing the actions of each sub-unit in turn, disregarding their exact timing. Different parts of Vlissingen were given codenames better suited to English or Scots tongues than the Dutch street names. Both are used to help reconcile contemporary accounts with today's street plan. The six troops of 4 Commando fanned out from the beachhead as follows:

No. 1 and No. 2 moved outwards along the seafront to expand the flanks of the beachhead: No. 1 moved left as far as the old Arsenaal or WINCHESTER, a thick-walled brick building to seaward of the Vissershaven; No. 2 went right, bypassing TROON, north of the street now known as Commandoweg, to seal off FALMOUTH, the spit of land between the sea and harbour.

No. 3 touched down at 0640hrs, moving quickly round the north side of the Vissershaven along Nieuwendijk towards Bellamypark or BRAEMAR, a 200-yard-long (180m) open space leading into the town from Koopmanshaven. Ignoring random Germans on the way, they reached Bellamypark about 0700hrs, as it became light. Clearing a pillbox there with the loss of two killed, they pushed on past the Western Harbour behind the buildings fronting the sea, towards their next objective, the naval barracks at HOVE. This whole line of buildings along Boulevard de Ruijter formed one long fortified barracks, blocked up in front and connected by a tunnel under the promenade. This heavily defended area brought the commandos to a stop, pending reinforcements.

No. 4, the heavy weapons troop, had to salvage one of their two 3in. mortars when their LCA was sunk by German crossfire; nevertheless they soon came into action, while the two medium machine-gun teams moved up Walstraat to the crossroads at Betje Wolffplein or BEXHILL.

The heavily restored Arsenaal is now a children's play centre, hence the pirate climbing out of the window, while the Vissershaven has become a marina. (Photo © Richard Brooks)

No. 5 also had a wet landing, with several men wounded, before following No. 3 Troop through Bellamypark to attack WORTHING, a pre-war bombproof barracks near the Gevangentoren on the seafront, sometimes known to the British as the Martello Tower.

No. 6 was led by Captain Nahuijs along Wilhelmina and Walstraat to BEXHILL, joining the machine-gunners in time to stop a series of German counterattacks channelled along Badhuisstraat by the Spuikom Lake.

4 KOSB disembarked at 0730hrs under increasing mortar and machine-gun fire, losing their battalion wireless sets as they did so. One LCA of the last wave was lost with all 26 men on board. Nevertheless the divisional Vickers guns and mountain howitzers landed safely, before German heavy artillery, probably batteries 5/202 at Domburg and 8/202 at Dishoek, brought down a curtain of fire across the estuary, cutting off further reinforcements. This was perhaps the most hazardous moment of *Infatuate I*. Wireless contact with brigade headquarters at Breskens and between companies had been lost, enemy mortar fire was accurate, and snipers were everywhere. Companies kept in touch by shouting, and blasts on a hunting horn.

Nevertheless, the battalion cleared the beach by 0800hrs, pushing outwards to reinforce the fragile perimeter. A Company went through No. 2 Troop at FALMOUTH to silence German positions on the spit. B and C turned left, hoping to push on into the New Town beyond the shipyard gates, but got no further than BEXHILL. Enemy positions beyond the crossroads were proof against infantry weapons, and too close to be shelled by guns beyond the Schelde. They were eventually dealt with by Typhoon fighter-bombers firing rockets. D Company, in battalion reserve, went to relieve the commandos around WORTHING. No. 5 Troop then moved on to their next objective at DOVER, another strongpoint on the seafront at the top of Coosje Buskenstraat. Looking down an appreciable slope from the top of the dyke, DOVER dominated BEXHILL. Its four-barrelled 2cm Flak complicated the difficulties of troops trying to get over the crossroads, nicknamed 'Hellfire Corner', into the New Town beyond.

The crisis of the battle was over by 1100hrs. The BEXHILL blocking position stopped the Germans from reinforcing their isolated positions in the Old Town, particularly at BRIGHTON, the Napoleonic bastion by the Western Harbour, or at HOVE and WORTHING. The mountain battery landed soon after 1100hrs, losing one gun and detachment whose LCA took a direct hit. The other seven howitzers were manhandled ashore in pieces, quickly assembled, and run up the street with drag ropes to engage machine-

TOP LEFT
The Oranjedijk from the Breskens ferry: the first landings were on the point just below the Oranjemolen. Follow-up troops landed on Uncle Beach, to the right of the mill, now covered by a grass-topped dyke. (Photo © Richard Brooks)

TOP RIGHT
The Oranjemolen and the beach where the first British troops landed, showing the height of the sea wall they had to scale. A German machine-gun position covered the beach from this point, but the Allied bombardment kept the defenders underground. (Photo © Richard Brooks)

BOTTOM
Entrance to the type 143 artillery observation bunker near the Oranjemolen, the first German position to fall into British hands. The saucer shape on the roof is the top of its armoured observation cupola, which gives an excellent view across the Schelde Estuary. (Photo © Richard Brooks)

gun nests over open sights. Lieutenant-Colonel Dawson called in air and artillery support at will. Bad weather at RAF bases in Belgium prevented air support until late morning, but from then onwards Typhoons and Spitfires flew a total of 152 sorties against German positions in Vlissingen. The artillery never failed, despite German jamming and the deleterious effects of wet weather on wireless batteries.

Heavy fighting went on all day. German naval war diaries report continual fighting in the harbour, shipyard and town, counterattacks launched against the landing area, combined with a strong terrorist presence – meaning Resistance fighters and civilians, who came out to welcome their liberators. The bombproof barracks underneath the Gevangentoren was cut off at 1056hrs, and it came to close fighting, presumably as D Company made their presence felt, and No. 5 Troop cut in between WORTHING and DOVER. HOVE and WORTHING had both fallen by noon, although the British front line remained stuck along Coosje Buskenstraat. The Kriegsmarine were surprised at the enemy's rapid advance against such strong defences, and embarrassed by the uselessness of their offshore minefields against shallow-

draft landing craft. Later in the afternoon 5 KOSB successfully crossed the Schelde, to reinforce the bridgehead, followed by 7/9 Royal Scots. Brigadier McLaren of 155th Brigade came ashore at 2200hrs, taking over from Lt. Col. Dawson. The British grip on Vlissingen was unlikely to be shaken off.

INFATUATE II: THE LANDING AT WESTKAPELLE

Where the Vlissingen landing relied on stealth, that at Westkapelle smashed its way ashore with an overwhelming mass of 182 ships and craft, and 200 amphibious vehicles. Force 'T' had assembled at Ostend on 27 October, vehicles embarked on the 30th, and troops on the 31st. The Support Squadron cleared harbour that afternoon, the remainder following after dark. The passage was calm and uneventful, Westkapelle's lighthouse coming into sight at 0700hrs next morning.

There were three landing beaches, one either side of Westkapelle and one inside the gap. From left to right these were:

TARE RED: the sea wall on the gap's northern shoulder, 800 yards (720m) wide with a 1 in 6 gradient, obstructed by wooden stakes, hedgehogs, and scattered masonry.

TARE WHITE: the gap itself, 380 yards across at high tide (340m); flat beaches either side heavily cratered and littered with debris, including an active if lopsided pillbox in the middle.

TARE GREEN: a sandy beach 450 yards south of the gap and 350 yards wide (400m and 310m), gradients of 1 in 9 to 1 in 6, backed by steep-faced dunes sown with mines; to be opened later for supply.

The outline plan was for *Warspite* and the monitors to bombard W15 and W13, the batteries nearest Westkapelle, lifting to W17 and W11 on the flanks. The Support Squadron would then engage targets along the beaches, forming two groups – one either side of the gap. Individual support craft were allocated as follows:

Type	Northern flank	Southern flank	Total
LCF	36, 38, 42	32, 35, 37	6 craft
LCG(L)	1, 2, 17	9, 10, 11	6 craft
LCG(M)	101	102	2 craft
LCH	98	269	2 craft
LCS(L)	254, 259, 260	252, 256, 258	6 craft
LCT(R)	331, 378, 457	334, 363	5 craft

While the LCG(L)s fired on W15 and W13, the LCFs and LCT(R)s drenched the intervening defences with small-calibre fire and rockets. The LCG(M)s were to beach, one either side of the gap, and engage pillboxes at point-blank range, closely supported by the more manoeuvrable LCS(L)s.

Covered by this fire, three troops of 41 (RM) Commando were to land from LCI(S)s on the northern shoulder (Red Beach), supported by the Flails and AVREs of the armoured assault teams. Five minutes later, the rest of 41 plus 10 Commando's Belgian and Norwegian Troops would land in amphibians launched from LCTs at the northern end of White Beach, and push north to secure the left flank of the beachhead. Meanwhile, 48 (RM)

Commando were to land south of the gap, at the right-hand end of White Beach, seize the radar station on the southern edge of the gap and push south to Zouteland, taking W13 on the way. Pugsley wanted their leading wave to land from LCI(S)s also, but Lt. Col. Moulton had unpleasant memories of using them in Normandy, and insisted on amphibians throughout. 47 (RM) Commando formed a floating reserve, intended to land south of the gap at H+60 minutes, pass through 48, clear the Dishoek dunes, and link up with 4 Commando west of Vlissingen at the Nolledijk Gap. Brigade headquarters and medical units were to land on White Beach, followed some time later by three LCTs with stores on Green. H-hour was at 0945hrs, four hours after the landing at Vlissingen, to combine the necessary conditions of tide and daylight. This sacrificed tactical surprise, although the use of landing craft to launch amphibians provided a compensating measure of technical surprise.

The final decision to proceed with the operation was taken barely an hour earlier. The weather in the North Sea in November is predictable only in that three days out of four the sea is too rough for landing craft. Calm usually meant fog, with negative consequences for air support and artillery observation. Ramsay and Simonds, therefore, delegated the decision to Pugsley and Leicester, the men on the spot. At 0600hrs on D-day, First Canadian Army passed on the RAF's meteorological assessment that no air support or spotting was likely, because of poor airfield conditions. Off Westkapelle, however, there was every indication that weather in the assault area would be suitable. Sea conditions were moderate, with no swell, cloud base 2,500ft (760m), and visibility 10–15 miles (15–22km). Shortly after 0800hrs the bombardment squadron opened fire, temporarily silencing W15. Twelve Typhoons appeared overhead from airfields in Belgium, unaffected by fog. Just after 0830hrs Pugsley made the signal 'Nelson', the codeword for the assault to go in. Had he not done so, the consequences for the troops already committed at Vlissingen might have been dire.

Neither the bombardment squadron nor the artillery at Breskens enjoyed much success. The latter's fire plan included 350 rounds of 155mm on W15 and 480 super-heavy rounds on W13, but Captain Sellars, Commander SSEF, saw little of this and POWs did not mention it. Later that day, the gunners were instructed to add 200 yards (180m) to ranges measured on the 1/25,000 maps, as their fire was falling consistently short. On the naval side, turret failure silenced HMS *Erebus* for 90 minutes. *Warspite* fired 353 rounds throughout the day in an inconclusive duel with W17, scoring no direct hits. The one bright spot for naval gunnery was HMS *Roberts*. About 0930hrs she achieved direct hits on W15, killing 30 German gunners and silencing two 3.7in. guns, perhaps the decisive moment of the landing. In the absence of observation aircraft from England, long-range fire against W13 was ineffective. The 15cm guns there continued to engage the Support Squadron with deadly effect.

The SSEF deployed 5 miles (8km) off the beach at 0848hrs, as it came under fire from W13. Half an hour later the German batteries scored their first hit on LCF 37, 2 miles (3km) offshore and still outside the range of its own light guns. Nevertheless, the ill-protected support craft gallantly pressed home their attack, hoping to divert the German batteries if they could not silence them. The LCS(L)s north of the gap survived by zigzagging at high speed, until LCS(L) 260 had to be towed out with her engines on fire. The LCS(L)s to the south were all lost, along with LCG(M) 102. Rescue craft picked up a single survivor from all four.

LCG(M) 101 beached at 0945hrs, and scored 15 direct hits on pillbox W267 to no effect, the 17-pdrs penetrating just halfway through its 10-foot-thick (3m) walls. Both guns out of action, she retracted from the beach, heeled over, and sank at 1025hrs. Remarkably most of the 35 men on board survived. Two were killed, and all four wounded were saved. Meanwhile the LCT(R)s launched their rockets, mostly covering their targets, except for LCT(R) 378, whose rockets fell short among the other support craft. The three northern LCT(R)s then reloaded with smoke, and laid a ragged screen for the incoming landing craft. The two southern LCT(R)s were both hit, one towing the other to safety. All three of the northern LCG(L)s were hit, and one of the southern group.

The remaining support craft and the approaching landing craft were saved by chance. At 1017hrs, after firing 200 rounds per gun, W13 fell silent, having apparently run out of ammunition. The AORG Report claimed this was the

An LCG(L) making smoke during the Support Squadron's run towards Westkapelle. Only one LCG(L) escaped from Walcheren undamaged. The main armament of 4.7in. guns is mounted singly in two turrets amidships. (Photo © Trustees of the Royal Marines Museum)

Infatuate II: assault on Westkapelle

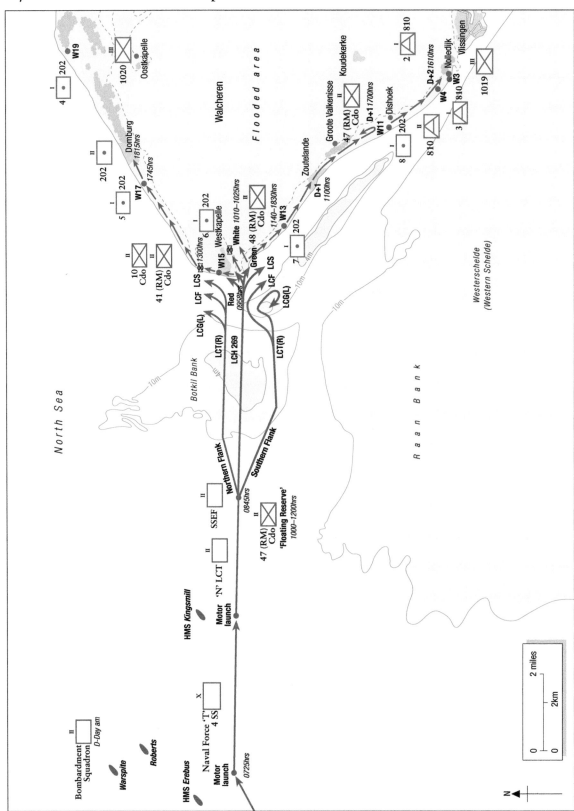

decisive moment of the action. Without this lucky accident, the battery would have finished off the support craft, and gone on to sink the troop-carrying landing craft. The report blamed poor German fire discipline, 'their grave tactical error of using up the ammunition on the support craft to which they were clearly not vulnerable, instead of holding their fire for use on the landing craft, the important targets'. Kriegsmarine reports, however, make no distinction between types of landing craft, referring generally to *Landungsfahrzeuge* and *Landungsboote*. Ship recognition was not a German strongpoint. Spurious sightings included a King George V-class battleship, six cruisers and four American battleships, identified from their alleged lattice masts. It seems most likely the gunners just fired on the nearest targets in range, i.e. the Support Squadron.

The Germans claimed 12 or 13 landing craft destroyed, which was not far wrong. Total SSEF losses out of 27 craft engaged were:

Type	Destroyed	Unfit for action	Damaged	Undamaged	In action
LCF	37, 38	32, 35, 36	42	–	1 craft
LCG(L)	1, 2	11, 17	10	9	2 craft
LCG(M)	101, 102	–	–	–	–
LCH	–	–	98	269	2 craft
LCS(L)	252, 256, 258	260	–	254, 259	2 craft
LCT(R)	–	334, 363	–	331, 378, 457	3 craft
Total	9 craft	8 craft	3 craft	7 craft	10 craft

Only five of the ten remaining craft had any offensive capability. Two were unarmed LCHs and three were LCT(R)s with no rockets. Of the crews, 172 were killed and 125 wounded out of 1,030 engaged, a shocking 29 per cent. Casualties would have been higher still but for three empty LCI(S)s taken along as fast rescue craft. Two of these were themselves damaged by mines while picking up survivors.

As fog cleared from Belgian airfields, rocket-firing Typhoons added their fire to that of the depleted SSEF. Initially the aircraft were directed to attack targets as soon as the LCT(R)s had discharged their salvoes. Subsequently squadrons went in at roughly five-minute intervals, starting with targets in the assault area, and shifting away as the commandos went ashore. The SSEF's surviving craft withdrew at 1230hrs, once the troops were firmly established ashore. Later that afternoon, a 'crocks' convoy of damaged support craft and empty LCTs sailed for Ostend.

The beneficiaries of the SSEF's sacrifice were the Royal Marine commandos, who landed with relatively few casualties. The assault craft approached in five waves, each consisting of a left and right component, planned to touch down at the times shown:

	Beach	Time	Left	Right
1	Red	H-hour	4 x LCTs: Flails and AVREs	3 x LCS(I)s: 41 Cdo B, P, S Tps
2	White	H+5 mins	2 x LCTs: 41 Cdo A, HQ, X Tps	3 x LCTs: 48 Cdo B, X, Y Tps
3	White	H+25 mins	3 x LCTs: 41 Cdo Y Tp & 10 Cdo	2 x LCTs: 48 Cdo A, Z Tps
4	White	H+60 mins	2 x LCTs: 4 SS Brigade Tac HQ	4 x LCTs: 47 Cdo
5	White	Discretionary	2 x LCTs: 4 SS Brigade Main HQ	4 x LCTs: miscellaneous (*)

(*) RE Field companies, medical units, pioneers, and additional RN Beach personnel.

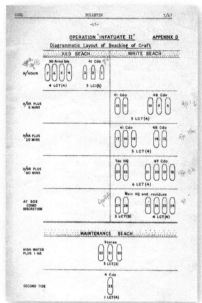

Scheduled landing times were thrown out by the accidents characteristic of amphibious warfare. The three leading LCI(S)s slowed down, thinking the LCTs were running late. They were then delayed themselves, first by LCT(R) 378's rockets causing them to swerve, and secondly by German shellfire. Consequently they touched down 13 or 27 minutes late, depending on the source. Naval reports give the time as 0958hrs; 41 (RM) Commando's War Diary and the AORG Report as 1012hrs. Once the LCI(S)s had beached, German guns could not depress sufficiently to hit them, allowing the commandos to scramble ashore in good order, and the wounded to be made comfortable before extraction. On the way out, however, one caught fire and blew up following hits on her high-octane fuel tanks. There was no opposition from enemy infantry. B Troop occupied the edge of the dyke, covering the western edge of Westkapelle. P Troop moved northwards to engage W15 with small-arms fire. S Troop set up its machine guns to suppress any fire directed from the southern edge of the village at subsequent landings in the gap.

The armoured assault teams did less well. Intending to beach simultaneously, in the event they approached in successive pairs. One of the leading craft was hit repeatedly. One shell brought down an AVRE bridge on top of the Flail tank in front; another set fire to the other AVRE's fascine. A naval rating was killed, and several sailors and commandos wounded. One of the second pair of LCTs came alongside to put out the fire, but damage to the leading craft's vehicles was so extensive she was ordered back to Ostend. Meanwhile, the second leading LCT came under fire from W15's 3in. guns as she approached Red Beach. Several naval personnel were killed or wounded, her captain taking her out again, lest all her vehicles were destroyed.

Red Beach was plainly too hot to use, so the second pair of first wave LCTs went into White Beach instead, joined by the survivor of the first pair. The last one touched down at 1100hrs, an hour and a quarter after the planned time. Instead of landing on the solid masonry of the sea wall, the Assault Teams found themselves stuck in the loose rubble that overlay the soft clay of the gap. The first AVRE ashore bellied and stuck fast, the LCT

retracting and beaching again a little further to the right. Both its Flails, the command Sherman and D7 armoured bulldozer made it into the village, but the second AVRE's bridge was shot away, leaving it stuck onboard. From a second LCT, one AVRE, one Flail and the command Sherman reached the village, leaving the D7 on the beach and one flail trapped under the other AVRE's bridge. From the third LCT nothing left the beach. The total survivors of this sapper disaster were: two Shermans, three Flails, two AVREs and one D7. The rising tide drowned all nine vehicles left on the beach, despite their crews working up to their necks in cold sea water to free them, under continual shell and mortar fire.

The delay in reaching White Beach brought the first wave ashore amidst the second and third waves. Weasels and Buffaloes milled about seeking a way off the beach, while two LVTs loaded with ammunition blazed fiercely. The second wave of 41 (RM) Commando landed at 1005hrs on the north shoulder of the gap without being hit. A Troop proceeded along the southern edge of the village, without opposition until they reached the eastern end of Zuidstraat. Fired on from the tower, they replied with small arms and PIATs, and requested support from the first of the tanks to reach the top of the dyke. According to 79th Armoured Division, direct hits were scored, flames broke out, and the defenders ran out to surrender amidst a shower of bricks. According to the troop commander, a German-speaking commando called on the garrison to come out, after which he himself climbed the narrow spiral staircase to take the surrender of the observation post at the top.

Tanks then moved along the main street, ploughing through rubble and barricades, seeking a position from which support fire could be brought down to help 48 (RM) Commando's advance along the dunes to the south-east. Flooded craters in the roads made this extremely difficult but eventually two gun tanks were put in position ready to open fire if called. Meanwhile 41's B and X Troops, following in echelon behind A Troop, cleared the rest of the town, and concentrated back preparatory to further moves. The remaining troop of 41 plus both of 10 Commando's touched down between 1015 and 1035hrs, mostly as planned. One LCT ran against some iron stakes, preventing its LVTs from disembarking, so No. 4 Troop's Belgians swam ashore. The LCT subsequently took ten hits from shellfire and sank, so their soaking was not entirely pointless.

The first wave of 48 (RM) Commando was shelled on the way in, but suffered no hits. It beached at 1010hrs, everyone landing dryshod. B and X Troops quickly overran their objectives: two wrecked pillboxes on the south

LANDING CRAFT OFF WALCHEREN (pp. 44–45)

Approaching Westkapelle's White Beach **(1)** about 1000hrs on D-Day, 1 November 1944, an LCT of *Infatuate II*'s second wave passes a hard-hit support craft **(2)**.

LCG(M) 101 was one of two support craft purposely designed to engage German beach defences at point-blank range with the 17-pdr anti-tank guns mounted in their two offset turrets. Gun platform stability was enhanced by 'flooding down' on the beach, by filling special tanks with sea water. Not one of the shells fired by LCG(M) 101's Royal Marine gun detachments missed their target, a pillbox north of the landing beach. Immobilized on the hostile shore, however, the craft made an easy target for German direct-fire weapons taking the beach in enfilade. Neither of the LCG(M)s committed at Walcheren survived their first operation. LCG(M) 102 was burnt out and lost with all 41 hands. Riddled with holes along her port side, LCG(M) 101 retracted from the beach using her kedge anchor, but sank stern first half a mile offshore. Remarkably only two of her crew were lost, killed by machine-gun fire while working the kedge. All the rest were saved, thanks to the calm and discipline of her complement of sailors and marines, who can be seen aft of the starboard turret, unrolling a life-raft and bringing the wounded up on deck.

Men of 41 (RM) Commando watch the unfolding drama from the bow of their LCT, as it heads towards the beach at a steady 6 knots **(3)**. They are wearing their trademark green berets, and, over their battledress, newly issued camouflaged Denison smocks. These were identical to those used by British airborne forces, becoming widespread amongst commandos during the winter of 1944–45. Weapons and personal equipment are stowed in the amphibious Buffalo LVTs behind them, lined up in the centre of the LCT's hold **(4)**, almost hidden beneath their complement of waiting marines. The LCT/LVT combination was a winner, allowing landing craft to drop their hinged ramp **(5)** directly on the beach, or offshore in shallow water, the LVTs carrying the assault troops ashore dryshod, with equipment and tactical units intact.

Little can be seen of Walcheren's low-lying coast, except for the Westkapelle lighthouse **(6)** which stands out above the smokescreen released by the defenders, and rolling along the dyke top before the north-west wind. Further left, a 15in. shell from the Bombardment Squadron bursts over battery W15 **(7)**. Hidden by the dust of the bombardment, its gun emplacements were one of the first objectives of the commandos once ashore. Deadly to LCG(M) 101, they would fall soon after midday, in barely two hours' time.

shoulder of the gap, and the radar station. The second wave touched down at 1025hrs, receiving shellfire attracted by the previous wave. One LCT was badly hit, wrecking the machine-gunners' LVT, killing its crew and starting an ammunition fire. More LVTs were brewed up on the beach, or mined while seeking shelter inshore of the dunes. Otherwise, the advance went well. By 1115hrs, the commandos had secured a footing in the south dunes, ready to proceed with their second task – the destruction of W13.

The fourth and fifth waves seem to have overlapped, unloading between 1045 and 1220hrs. More LVTs were hit on the beach or blew up on mines. Brigade tactical headquarters landed in Westkapelle at noon, but subsequently crossed the gap under shellfire to establish itself in the radar station and nearby concrete bunkers. 47 (RM) Commando spent the morning 6 miles (10km) offshore, watching support craft explode or float past bottom up. Orders to land came at 1230hrs, after missing the optimum tidal conditions. In the last few hundred yards of the run in, shells hit three out of their four LCTs. Instead of beaching south of the gap as planned, they lowered their ramps to swim off

TOP
A Flail tank leaves LCT 737 during Bramble's second attempt to beach. The vehicle reached Westkapelle despite the mud and rubble in the foreground, only to be drowned by the rising tide. (Photo © Trustees of the Royal Marines Museum)

BOTTOM
Men from 41 (RM) Commando advance down Westkapelle's devastated Zuidstraat to evict German artillery observers from the lighthouse tower. The commandos are wearing the Denison smocks specially issued for Operation *Infatuate*. (Photo © Trustees of the Royal Marines Museum)

6 ● MAA 202

RANGEFINDER

W15

WESTKAPELLE

RED

10 Cdo

LAYCOCK

EVENTS

1 Three LCI(S)s extract after landing the covering party from 41 (RM) Commando on the Westkapelle dyke at 0958hrs. Meanwhile the first wave of four LCTs struggles to land the armoured assault teams' flails and AVREs on Red Beach.

2 Five LCTs land the main body of 41 (RM) Commando and the first flight of 48 on White Beach, either side of the gap, at 1010hrs.

3 The surviving support craft continue to draw German fire away from the troop-carrying landing craft.

4 Five LCTs carrying 10 (Inter-Allied) Commando and remaining troops of 41 and 48 (RM) Commandos approach White Beach.

5 A Troop, 41 (RM) Commando, clears Westkapelle main street and captures the German observation post in the lighthouse tower, while B and X Troops fan out through the town.

6 B and X Troops of 48 (RM) Commando clear White Beach, and capture the German radar station beyond, before setting off down the dunes for the coastal battery at W13.

7 Y and P Troops of 41 (RM) Commando storm the German coastal battery at W15 about 1230hrs, supported by No. 5 Troop of 10 (Inter-Allied) Commando.

ASSAULT LANDING AT WESTKAPELLE, 1 NOVEMBER 1944

The assault on Westkapelle went in just before 1000hrs, the defenders distracted by the Support Squadron's self-sacrificial diversion. 48 (RM) Commando landed south of the gap, and rapidly pushed south, while 41 (RM) and 10 (Inter-Allied) Commandos assaulted Westkapelle itself. By early afternoon the town and the German battery at W15 were both safely in Allied hands.

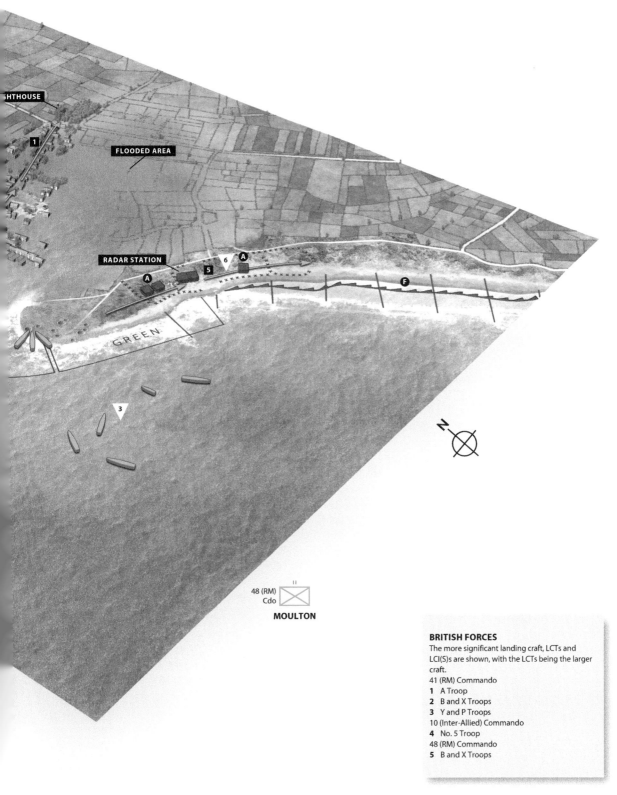

Note: Map area is approx 1.8 x 2.2 km

LIGHTHOUSE

FLOODED AREA

RADAR STATION

GREEN

48 (RM) Cdo

MOULTON

BRITISH FORCES
The more significant landing craft, LCTs and LCI(S)s are shown, with the LCTs being the larger craft.
41 (RM) Commando
1   A Troop
2   B and X Troops
3   Y and P Troops
10 (Inter-Allied) Commando
4   No. 5 Troop
48 (RM) Commando
5   B and X Troops

the amphibians in the middle. Several hits on the rightmost LCT, carrying Commando headquarters, started a brisk fire amongst the LVTs and some Weasels loaded with flame-throwers. HQ and Heavy Weapons Troops drove ashore all right, but the occupants of the other three LVTs had to swim. The remaining three LCTs drifted to port, left of the gap, where they bunched in a disorderly fashion. Q Troop landed correctly to the south; A Troop, distributed amongst the different LCTs, and X Troop landed to the north; Y Troop landed to the south, but then followed the troop commander's Buffalo northwards across the gap.

It was dark before 47 re-assembled south of the gap. Many of its marines were without weapons, and soaked from floundering about Westkapelle, trying to re-cross the gap on foot. The CO blamed the late timing of the order to land, when the Support Squadron had shot its bolt. The Commando could easily have landed sooner, escaping the attention of the German guns: 'A reserve', he commented acidly, 'is not of much use if it has lost its edge'.

STORMING THE BATTERIES I: ZUIDERDUIN AND DOMBURG

Three of the four great batteries that prevented Allied vessels entering the Westerschelde would be in British hands by the end of D-day. North of the gap, 41 (RM) Commando captured W15 soon after landing, pressing on to take Domburg and W17 in the late afternoon. Meanwhile in the Zuiderduin, the south dunes, 48 (RM) Commando stormed W13 in a dramatic set-piece battle. The Allied intention was to clear the south-west coast first, as lying nearest to the shipping lanes. The task of British troops to the north was to form a covering position whilst this was done. Once that had been done, the pace of progress there would depend on events to the south of the gap.

The first battery to fall was W15 or Marineküstenbatterie Westkapelle, held by Kriegsmarine battery 6/202. Hard hit by HMS *Roberts* earlier in the day, W15 could still fire one of its casemated 3.7in. guns, and both the 3in. ones from their open emplacements. On Westkapelle's northern outskirts, barely a kilometre from the gap, it was much too close for comfort. W15's fire against incoming vessels had been deadly, sinking three support craft and an LCT, stopping the armoured assault teams from landing on Red Beach, and causing 120–130 naval casualties. It had also shelled landing craft bound across the Schelde for Vlissingen, cutting off urgently needed reinforcements. Its capture was an immediate priority. The forces available were 41 (RM) Commando, plus two troops of 10 Commando, some engineers and whatever armour might make it off the beach.

Most of Westkapelle was clear of Germans by 1115hrs. North-west of the town, however, P Troop of 41 (RM) Commando was held up by heavy small-arms fire from W15's local defences. Colonel Palmer went forward with Y Troop's commander to reconnoitre a way round to the right, along the edge of the floods. A plan was agreed whereby P would act as fire troop to Y Troop moving round the inland flank, the two troops arranging a smoke and fire programme between them. Y Troop attacked at noon, and, according to British accounts, had captured the battery with 120 POWs by 1230hrs.

Meanwhile, the Norwegians of 10 Commando had secured the northern part of Westkapelle. Seeing 41 (RM) Commando attacking across open ground to landward, they advanced through the sand dunes next the sea to seize a tactically advantageous position on 41's left, from where they kept

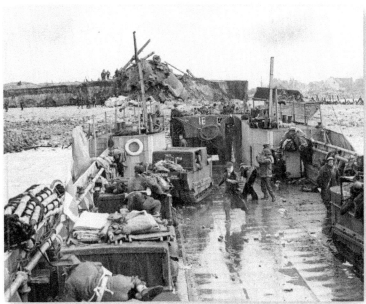

the defenders' heads down. The battery's final wireless message, timed at 1255hrs, reported the enemy just 110 yards (100m) from the command post. Closely engaged by infantry, the battery fought on until regimental headquarters at Domburg reported its final capture at 1355hrs.

The varied times reported may reflect the extended areas fought over, as well as erratic timekeeping. The individual positions making up a German strongpoint were dispersed over a considerable area. The barbed wire around W15 enclosed a space some 600 yards long (550m). Within this, isolated snipers might hold out for some time after the main positions had fallen. While the Belgians dealt with the former, the Norwegians consolidated the latter, hanging out a Norwegian flag one of them had brought ashore. Established in a concrete gun house, 10 Commando Headquarters had a practical demonstration of its defensive value that night, surviving a direct hit of unknown origin without casualties.

Thus established across the northern approaches to Westkapelle, 10 Commando provided a firm base for the continued advance of Y and P Troops. These pressed on another 300 yards (250m) to mop up a further enemy position around the Noorderhoofd lighthouse, where the coast turns north-east. This formed a natural point for the British to pause, only a narrow neck of sand dunes separating the sea from the floods. Under pressure from II Canadian Corps to press the advance south of the gap, the brigade commander directed that no further advance north of the lighthouse should take place until further orders. The immediate need for further progress was alleviated by a prophylactic air strike on W17. Throughout the whole period starting with the seizure of the town, naval battery 5/202 of Marineküstenbatterie Domburg had been shelling the beachhead with its 22cm guns. Fighter-bombers were now called for, and delivered a successful attack that silenced the battery for a time.

South of the gap, 48 (RM) Commando's first three troops had pushed on at speed, engaging in a running fight with small parties of enemy who appeared sporadically from the numerous concrete and earth works along the dunes. At 1140hrs 48 (RM) Commando made contact with W13,

D-DAY AT WESTKAPELLE (pp. 52–53)

A Royal Marine commando **(1)** watches amphibious vehicles stream ashore from a Landing Craft Tank (LCT) at Westkapelle, shortly after 1030hrs on 1 November 1944. The British deployed a mass of machines to overcome the obstacles they expected to encounter on Walcheren's beaches. Many of these were lost, more to difficult landing conditions than German resistance. Final success came down to the courage and infantry skills of the individual soldiers.

When all went well, the assaulting troops landed dry-shod. Rifle troops rode in Landing Vehicles Tracked or LVTs. Known as 'Buffaloes' **(2)**, these weighed in at around 18 tons, and could carry up to 30 men. Their 20mm Polson cannon and Browning machine guns could have delivered a hail of suppressive fire, if German infantry had defended the beaches in strength.

Command elements, such as signallers and artillery observation parties, travelled in the unarmoured M29C Weasel **(3)**. Exerting little ground pressure, these could easily slither across the treacherous mud and rubble that covered the landing beaches. They proved underpowered and unstable, however, crossing the tidal waters of the Westkapelle Gap. Many were swamped and lost, together with their precious loads.

The Assault Vehicle Royal Engineers (AVRE) was at the other end of the spectrum to the Weasel **(4)**. Adapted from the Churchill tank, AVREs were armed with a petard mortar to blast a way through German defences, and featured extended exhausts and air intakes for wading ashore. Agile for its 40 tons, the vehicle was too heavy for conditions on White Beach. Once their tracks had bitten down through the rubble, they sank into the underlying clay, and stuck fast, as here. Only two out of the six AVREs put ashore at Westkapelle made it safely off the beach.

The LCT was a war-winning invention, allowing Allied tanks to accompany infantry across fire-swept beaches **(5)**. Those here are LCTs Mark 4, capable of carrying five LVTs and six Weasels, or an armoured assault team of six tanks and armoured bulldozers. One LCT has successfully discharged its LVTs, while another **(6)** turns away from the beach under fire. One of its AVREs is still onboard, betrayed by the box girder bridge sticking up amidships.

Active resistance to the landings at Westkapelle consisted mainly of artillery fire from German coastal batteries. Their accurate fire prevented armoured assault teams landing on Red Beach as planned, and inflicted heavy losses amongst vehicles and landing craft. These could have been still heavier had the gunners fired high-explosive rounds instead of armour-piercing. In the absence of German infantry, however, the defences that littered the foreshore **(7)** were rapidly circumvented. Obstacles are of little value, unless covered by fire.

Marineküstenbatterie Zoutelande, held by naval battery 7/202. Y Troop attacked without support to maintain the impetus of the advance, but resistance was stiffening. The attack failed, and the troop commander was killed. A properly coordinated attack was necessary, which took some hours to organize.

Dune fighting presented particular problems. The steep, loose sand made every movement laborious and time-consuming, eating into the short November afternoon. Weapons had to be cleaned continuously to keep them clear of clinging particles of sand and salt. German sub-machine guns worked better in such conditions than the American Thompson guns, and were greatly sought after. Impassable to the Weasels which carried the more powerful wireless sets, the dunes blanketed the lighter man-portable sets, forcing officers to plod up and down to give orders, or spy out the land for themselves. Casualties had to be evacuated and ammunition brought forward manually. The only advantage of the sand was its tendency to smother minefields, neutralizing a key element in the German defence.

The narrow frontage between sea and floods gave Col. Moulton few tactical choices. He left X Troop to hold the ground Y Troop had gained. Unaware of the Germans' ammunition shortage, he told his men to keep shooting at the observation tower to prevent the battery once more opening fire with its main armament. Z Troop was warned for the attack, while A Troop occupied a sandy spur in the flooded area on the left to provide flanking fire. Fire support was a problem: the support craft were nearly all out of action, the forward observation officer could not raise the artillery at Breskens, the Commando's own medium machine guns had been lost on landing and the tank liaison officer found it impossible to direct the fire of the Shermans at Westkapelle. The Royal Artillery FOB observing for HMS *Roberts* had been in touch with the ship since 1115hrs, but Capt. Pugsley, back in HMS *Kingsmill*, stopped her firing as the Commando approached the battery. Moulton had to go back to the beach to find a wireless powerful enough to arrange an artillery fire plan and air support. Meanwhile, the assault troops caught their breath, and cleaned their weapons.

A commando hurries captured Germans back down Zuidstraat at gunpoint. The unsubmissive prisoner in the centre appears to be pushing his luck. Overcoats and fibre suitcases were standard POW accessories. (Photo © Trustees of the Royal Marines Museum)

Moulton reached brigade headquarters about 1430hrs, and arranged a bombardment by two 5.5in. medium artillery regiments between 1545 and 1600hrs, firing intensely for the last five minutes. Then RAF fighter-bombers would strafe the battery for five minutes, 48 (RM) Commando marking the target with smoke from their 2in. mortars. The Commando would assault at 1605hrs, having got as near to the German positions as possible under cover of the fire plan. Returning to the front line at 1530hrs, Moulton found German mortar fire had thrown the whole plan into jeopardy: Z Troop was badly hit. All its officers and senior NCOs were casualties, the commander of X Troop, the FOB and medical officer all being killed. The only good news was that A Troop had spotted the mortar position, and shot the crew.

As 80lb shells began falling 200 yards (180m) ahead of the commandos' forward positions, B Troop was hastily substituted for Z Troop, moving up breathlessly through the steep, yielding sand. As the shelling stopped, the fighter-bombers came in so low that the waiting commandos could see the bombs leave the racks directly over their heads, sailing on to land in the battery. Eight Typhoons dropped 16 500lb bombs, and fired 2,030 rounds of 20mm cannon. They claimed two direct hits on a casemate, while the FOO and 48 (RM) Commando reported a bomb splitting one of the casemates open, smashing the 15cm gun and killing its crew. Prisoners later thought the damage was done by one of HMS *Roberts*'s 15in. shells, but few of these were fired at W13. Subsequent inspection of the damage suggested a low-level projectile, most likely a bomb, had entered the embrasure from in front.

The commandos were much closer to the air strike than the regulation safe distance, to make sure of entering the battery before the Germans could recover. B Troop advanced boldly through the minefield, and burst through the wire entanglement covered by smoke and A Troop's Bren guns on the flank. They silenced the command post by shooting into its observation slits, and reached the open back of the second gun casemate, compelling the gunners to surrender just as X Troop came up in support.

German accounts of the attack claimed the battery was closely engaged from about noon, the enemy pressing on the north flank, soon reaching the command post, which at 1354hrs reported many tanks (*sic*) in the position: 'The battery would finally be lost in the course of the afternoon (1600hrs?) through the silencing of the guns by mortar fire, and for want of support from the army'. Moulton might have thought the latter assessment unfair: it was the Kriegsmarine gunners who declined to mix it with the commandos in close fighting, while the infantry, veterans of the Eastern Front, were less inclined to give in.

W13's big guns were silent, but random fire still came from the far end of the battery, where a 2cm Flak Vierling fired occasional bursts overhead. As darkness fell, Y Troop patrolled forwards to find the main casemates empty, their guns blown up by the enemy. B Troop brought in 70 more POWs from accommodation bunkers on the landward side of the dunes, including the battery commander. By 1830hrs, the whole battery was secured, except the 2cm Flak. The Commando's vehicles were brewed up or stranded far behind, unable to get forwards through the sand and minefields. Everyone who could be spared spent the night carrying up food and ammunition, including the colonel. Casualties had been heavy. By the end of D+1, when it saw little fighting, the Commando's total losses amounted to 12 killed, 57 wounded, and 21 missing, 26 per cent in all. Most of the missing were found later on back in Ostend, evacuated by their stricken LCTs, but officer casualties were disproportionately high: six killed and three wounded.

Even before 48 (RM) Commando's attack, brigade was sufficiently satisfied by progress south of the gap to resume the advance on Domburg. Leaving A and S Troops in Westkapelle under command of 10 Commando to assist in its defence, 41 (RM) Commando advanced north-east along the dunes at 1500hrs. The frontage available was narrow, a couple of hundred yards between the sea and the floods inland, broadening out to two or three times that distance towards Domburg. Consequently, the Commando advanced on a one-troop front: Y Troop first, Commando headquarters, P, B, and X Troops following. The order of march changed from time to time, the Commando spreading out on a two-troop front during the final approach. P Troop led along the road on top of the dyke followed by B Troop, while X Troop moved out into the dunes right of the road, Y Troop continuing to follow B Troop. German accounts claim the advance was accompanied by tanks, but these were still entangled in Westkapelle, only reaching Domburg on D+1.

Details of fire support are scanty, although the FOO attached to 41 (RM) Commando was ashore by 1020hrs, and continued shooting all day with the 155mm batteries of 1, 51, and 59 Heavy Regiments. HMS *Warspite* engaged W17 at 1510hrs using a Royal Artillery Air Observation Post, their usual spotting aircraft still being grounded in Kent. The AOP, however, used different wavelengths and a different system for reporting fall of shot, and the shoot was ineffective. 84 Group's fighter-bombers did better. Twenty-four Spitfires appeared at 1600hrs, dropping 18 500lb bombs into W17, and strafing the battery with 20mm cannon and .5in. machine guns, which silenced it once more. Another 24 Spitfires attacked position W283 between Noorderhoofd and Domburg, hitting it with 23 500lb bombs and 10,000 20mm and .5in. rounds.

Every effort was made to speed the advance as darkness fell, but large parties of potentially hostile Germans came out to surrender, and got in the way. W17 and a smaller battery immediately inland surrendered about 1745hrs, without much of a fight, B Troop staying behind to mop up.

According to a prisoner it was *Warspite*'s ineffective 15in. shells that had completed the demoralization of the garrison, not the air strikes. The Kriegsmarine thought W17 was overrun at 1830hrs, attributing its fall to a broad outflanking movement on the British right, combined with the battery's inability to fight at close quarters, having no infantry support as usual. 21st Army Group remarked on W17's ineffectual resistance and poor shooting: Bomber Command had knocked out its fire-control tower and one of the four 22cm guns. Two more heavy guns suffered mechanical breakdowns, while prisoners from W15 complained of 'friendly fire' from W17's 15cm field howitzer, suggesting a general loss of control.

The commandos reached the main Domburg crossroads by 1815hrs. It was now quite dark, apart from the light of houses set on fire by HMS *Warspite*. P Troop went forwards with the second-in-command to establish contact with the enemy. A few stragglers were found, some of them drunk, but exploitation forward into the wooded country beyond appeared inadvisable before daylight. P Troop took up a covering position in the centre of town, Y Troop covering their right flank as far as the floods, with B Troop further back in reserve.

Marine-Artillerie Abteilung 202's command post, lying directly north-east behind the dunes on the edge of town, was abandoned under the pressure of the British advance at about the same time. Its final transmission was reported at 1900hrs, German times running behind the British to the end. The regimental commander and his men, joined by soldiers withdrawing from the Domburg battery, fell back north-eastwards to link up with battery 4/202 at Marineküstenbatterie Oostkapelle at W19.

Not all Germans had yet left Domburg's immediate area. At 1900hrs, X Troop reported an encounter with a determined party established on a commanding sand dune forwards of the main British position. The troop commander, who had been leading, was hit along with his marine orderly, their absence going unnoticed in the darkness when the troop withdrew to cover. Two patrols went forward to locate the wounded men, without success. B Troop went to help X Troop contain this isolated pocket of resistance, later exchanging shots with some diehards seeking to advance into town. Later still, the commanding officer went to see if the casualties could be rescued, but fires lit by the enemy in their immediate neighbourhood made all attempts to reach them quite useless. By the time the enemy withdrew north-eastwards along the dunes next morning, the troop commander had died, although his orderly was found alive.

Despite this sad conclusion to their first 24 hours in Walcheren, 41 (RM) Commando had done well, taking both of the northern batteries that posed a threat to Allied shipping and the brigade's continued advance down the south-west coast towards Vlissingen. The latter would be Leicester's priority for D+1, relative quiet descending upon the north-west.

CLEARING VLISSINGEN

The most complex part of the liberation of Walcheren was the clearance of Vlissingen. The town was a tangle of docks and narrow streets, many converted into fast-flowing rivers by the Schelde waters pouring through gaps in the dykes. Its defenders were ensconced in bunkers, cranes and warehouses, intermixed with a densely packed civilian population. Despite this, 155th (Lowland) Brigade took just two days to clear the town, and another to reduce the last centres of resistance in the Kernwerk, east of the inner harbour. There were three separate actions:

1) 4 Commando's capture of DOVER, the seafront strongpoint at the top of Coosje Buskenstraat on 2 November;
2) 5 KOSB's breakout into the New Town the same day, followed on 4 November by their advance across the Walcheren Canal into the dockside areas of HAYMARKET, STRAND and PICCADILLY;
3) 7/9 Royal Scots' nightmare battle for the Hotel Grand Britannia during the early hours of 3 November, when the battalion unexpectedly stormed the headquarters of Verteidigungsbereich Vlissingen, decapitating the German defence.

Close together physically, but separated by the compartmentalization characteristic of fighting in built-up areas, these will be described separately, in order.

Some of the destruction wrought during the battle for Vlissingen's fortified seafront: piles of rubble surround a type 502 accommodation bunker and civilian air-raid shelter near HOVE. In the background, St Jacob's Church and the dockyard cranes once occupied by German snipers. (Author's collection)

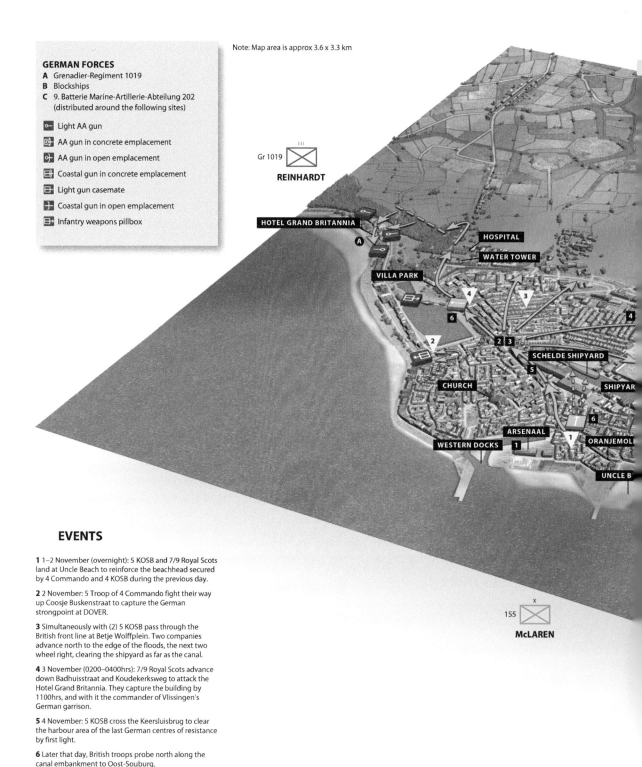

Note: Map area is approx 3.6 x 3.3 km

GERMAN FORCES

A Grenadier-Regiment 1019
B Blockships
C 9. Batterie Marine-Artillerie-Abteilung 202
(distributed around the following sites)

⊶ Light AA gun

▣ AA gun in concrete emplacement

⊶ AA gun in open emplacement

🗏 Coastal gun in concrete emplacement

🗏 Light gun casemate

✚ Coastal gun in open emplacement

🗏 Infantry weapons pillbox

Gr 1019 ⊠

REINHARDT

HOTEL GRAND BRITANNIA

A

HOSPITAL

WATER TOWER

VILLA PARK

4

3

6

4

2

2 3

SCHELDE SHIPYARD

5

CHURCH

SHIPYAR

6

ARSENAAL

1

WESTERN DOCKS

1

1

ORANJEMOL

UNCLE B

155 ⊠

McLAREN

EVENTS

1 1–2 November (overnight): 5 KOSB and 7/9 Royal Scots land at Uncle Beach to reinforce the beachhead secured by 4 Commando and 4 KOSB during the previous day.

2 2 November: 5 Troop of 4 Commando fight their way up Coosje Buskenstraat to capture the German strongpoint at DOVER.

3 Simultaneously with (2) 5 KOSB pass through the British front line at Betje Wolffplein. Two companies advance north to the edge of the floods, the next two wheel right, clearing the shipyard as far as the canal.

4 3 November (0200–0400hrs): 7/9 Royal Scots advance down Badhuisstraat and Koudekerksweg to attack the Hotel Grand Britannia. They capture the building by 1100hrs, and with it the commander of Vlissingen's German garrison.

5 4 November: 5 KOSB cross the Keersluisbrug to clear the harbour area of the last German centres of resistance by first light.

6 Later that day, British troops probe north along the canal embankment to Oost-Souburg.

BREAKOUT FROM THE VLISSINGEN BEACHHEAD

The battle for Vlissingen lasted for three days after the initial landings on 1 November. During D+1, 5 KOSB and 4 Commando broke out of the beachhead, securing most of the town; 7/9 Royal Scots went on to eliminate the German command bunker at the Hotel Grand Britannia early on D+2. The now leaderless defenders of the harbour area were mopped up by 5 KOSB next morning.

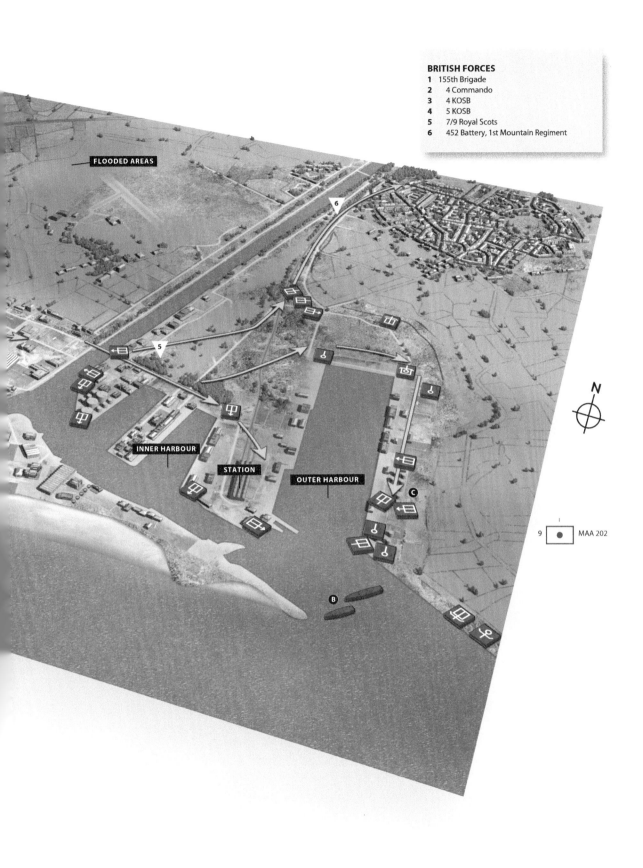

BRITISH FORCES
1 155th Brigade
2 4 Commando
3 4 KOSB
4 5 KOSB
5 7/9 Royal Scots
6 452 Battery, 1st Mountain Regiment

FLOODED AREAS

INNER HARBOUR

STATION

OUTER HARBOUR

N

9 ● MAA 202

The commandos resumed their attack at 0700hrs on D+1, after a noisy, cold and uncomfortable night. The Germans had resorted to rifle grenades and a flame-thrower, while the British shelled the seafront with heavy artillery. No. 5 Troop's progress up Coosje Buskenstraat towards DOVER was slow, a 2cm Flak Vierling commanding the street from the dyke top. One section gained the roof of the Alhambra Cinema, and engaged the strongpoint with their PIAT, while the other section dashed across the street. Both sections 'mouseholed' forwards on either side of the road, blowing holes through the garden walls of adjoining houses with prepared charges, as practised in Ostend. Closing in at midday, they pulled back to let half a dozen Typhoons strafe the position. German situation reports noted *Jabo-Angriff* at this time, 'fighter-bomber attacks', against the harbour blockships and anti-aircraft positions, 'heavy pressure against the Gevangentoren', and 'streetfighting in Vlissingen, particularly between the Boulevard and Water Tower', where lies Coosje Buskenstraat.

The French commandos finally reached the corner at the top of the street, overlooking their objective, about 1630hrs. Some of the defenders ran for it, and were shot as they went. No. 1 section fired PIAT bombs into DOVER's embrasures at close range, without apparently inspiring its inmates to surrender. As the commandos prepared to blow in the armoured door with a made-up charge, a white flag appeared, followed by three officers and 54 dazed German soldiers. Thoroughly shaken by the deluge of fire, their commander's main concern was to get away quickly, before his friends counterattacked along the boulevard. His captors promptly called down a prophylactic artillery barrage, after which commented 4 Commando's war diary: 'Nothing was ever seen of any counterattack'.

5th Battalion The King's Own Scottish Borderers disembarked in Vlissingen at 1700hrs on D-day, their earlier attempt to cross frustrated by a wall of shellfire across the Schelde. Billeted in the less damaged houses near brigade headquarters in the Arsenaal, they found Vlissingen quiet, barring a few snipers, its streets carpeted with broken glass, rubble and dead Germans. Large numbers of Dutch civilians were still about, several hundred escaping into British lines overnight using the floating bridge across the mouth of the shipyard dock. LCAs returning to Breskens carried numerous women and children to safety, as well as prisoners and wounded.

A battalion 'O' group at 2000hrs issued orders for the next day's breakout. Passing through 4 KOSB at BEXHILL, A and C Companies would advance north past the shipyard gates into the areas beyond Betje Wolffplein, codenamed GROUSE and COD. The companies crossed their start line at 0500hrs, following the usual softening-up of the enemy positions by field and medium artillery, with A Company leading. Mopping up behind them, C Company came under a spate of mortar bombs, suffering numerous casualties including the company commander.

452 Mountain Battery were called in to deal with an obstinate bunker built into the reservoir wall across the Spuikom. Indirect artillery fire proved useless, so the gunners borrowed the brigadier's Weasel to tow one of their howitzers across 'Hellfire Corner' and along Badhuisstraat to engage the target through a bedroom window. Dismantling the gun they carried it up the stairs of a house in pieces, to be reassembled behind drawn curtains. The wrench used to separate chase and breech was lost during the jolting tow across cobbled streets, so the whole piece, weighing over a quarter of a ton, had to be carried upstairs as a single item. In 20 minutes, it was ready to open fire at the enemy position 250 yards (220m) across the reservoir: 'The first round brought the ceiling down', recalled the Number One, 'and made us look like millers. Our second round hit two Germans who had decided to leave at that precise moment, and they were never seen again'. Eight rounds sufficed to persuade their friends to surrender, by which time the front of the house was falling off and parts of the trail poking through the floor into the room below.

The KOSB's leading companies took their objectives by noon, allowing B and D Companies to pass through on the right, into DUCK and TROUT, north of the dock. The dockyard area presented particular problems, with unexpected inlets of deep water pushing between shattered houses and workshops. The German deputy naval commander had reported the guns of Marineflakbatterie Ost 4/810 and Marineküstenbatterie Kernwerk 9/202 out of action the previous evening, but there were numerous well-defended bunkers in the harbour area, with a plentiful supply of ammunition. As their guns were silenced, the Kriegsmarine gunners were distributed as infantry

The Grand Hotel Britannia after 7/9 Royal Scots had finished with it. The lookout post of Seekommandant Vlissingen's type FL241 command bunker is on the right, carefully painted with false windows to resemble a harmless seaside villa. (Photo © Zeeuwse Bibliotheek/Beeldbank)

STREETFIGHTING IN VLISSINGEN (pp. 64–65)

British infantry dash across Bellamypark during the beachhead fighting of 1 November **(1)**. Codenamed BRAEMAR, Bellamypark was a dangerously open space, extending inland from the Merchant's Dock, of which it was once the continuation. Despite this, Bellamypark remained above the encircling floods, allowing British troops to advance quickly and dry-shod into the centre of Vlissingen.

German snipers are still active, so the group is well spread out, sprinting for shelter on the far side of the square. No. 3 Troop of 4 (Army) Commando had passed this way at first light, outflanking German machine-gunners in the building to the left **(2)**. Its relatively undamaged condition suggests the latter were taken by surprise, wrong-footed by the speed of the commandos' advance. Later in the morning, French commandos from No. 5 Troop and D Company of 4 KOSB crossed the café-fringed square to join the battle for HOVE and BRIGHTON, the heavily fortified positions on the seafront beyond the buildings opposite **(3)**.

The group depicted here may all be commandos, or perhaps a mixture of commandos in green berets and regular infantry wearing the Mark III 'turtle'-pattern helmets used by British troops throughout the North-west Europe campaign **(4)**. Less symmetrical than the World War I battle bowler, these were deeper at the back than the front, providing improved protection at the side and rear. All are wearing camouflaged

Denison smocks, which the Borderers kept when they lost their mountain warfare role. Wearing these over their battledress, they were practically indistinguishable from the commandos, as no badges were worn on the smocks. The visual ambiguity emphasizes the fluidity of British tactics in Vlissingen, where successive waves of troops flowed in to flesh out the skeleton beachhead seized by the first to arrive.

Weapons and equipment give away little. Personal weapons are all the standard British .303in.-calibre No. 4 Rifle, the mass-produced wartime version of the old short magazine Lee-Enfield **(5)**. Only two men have fixed their spike bayonets, a weapon used more for puncturing tins of condensed milk than Germans. The first three of the party have abandoned their haversacks for ease of movement, revealing their 1937-pattern webbing shoulder straps. The other two have adopted different approaches to carrying their rolled-up groundsheet, strapped over or underneath the haversack.

The brick-lined arch between the rearmost running men is a civilian air-raid shelter, not a bunker **(6)**. Vlissingen's docks and harbour facilities made the town an obvious target for aerial attack, and the occupying authorities organized the building of some 50 shelters independently of the military fortification programme. In the event, Vlissingen escaped heavy aerial bombardment, damage being concentrated along the seafront and around the dockyard.

among the strongpoints. Besides the usual mortar and machine-gun fire, suicide squads of snipers perched up high in the shipyard cranes. The 3.7in. pack howitzers proved invaluable against such targets, single guns engaging the snipers in a deadly duel. One round was usually enough to demolish a crane-driver's cabin, or bring the snipers' dead bodies hurtling down onto the quayside; 'like a rook shoot', said a watching infantryman. By dusk a large part of Vlissingen was cleared of Germans. Three companies of 5 KOSB held the line westwards from Keersluisbrug, the bridge where Prins Hendrikweg crosses the Walcheren Canal heading for the railway station, B Company at the bridge, with D Company behind their right flank in the shipyard.

Next day, 3 November, 5 KOSB was held up by continued resistance in the eastern parts of Vlissingen. They deployed a loudspeaker to invite the defenders to surrender, with mixed results. Some Germans came in, but B Company was shelled, and at 1415hrs the two right-hand companies withdrew 300 yards (270m) to allow counterbattery fire and rocket strikes by RAF Typhoons. Very early on 4 November, B and D Companies crossed the Walcheren Canal at the bridge: B Company pushed left to secure the railway embankment leading to Middelburg and the nearby German regimental aid post; D Company drove to the right, passing through HAYMARKET and STRAND, the two jetties between the canal and the two arms of the Binnenhaven, to secure the railway station at PICCADILLY. Despite enfilading fire from the north-eastern corner of the Buitenhaven or outer harbour, all companies had their objectives by 0530hrs. As it became light, C Company passed through them against considerable opposition from machine-gun and rifle fire to clear the shambles of bombed-out industrial facilities beyond. The PIATs were used to silence pillboxes, and Brens to cut down the fleeing defenders. Later that day A Company took over from C Company east of the large basin, while B Company probed north along the railway embankment, above the floodwater, towards Oost-Souburg.

Later the divisional commander complimented both his KOSB battalions. The 4th had successfully carried out an assault landing, 'right on the doorstep of what I believe to be the world's most strongly defended place'. The 5th had completed the job by mopping up an area riddled with pillboxes joined by underground passages: 'According to the rules of war, neither task should have been successful… their losses were exceedingly light in relation to the strength of their objectives.' Casualties for 5 KOSB at Vlissingen were nine killed and 53 wounded, a total of 62. 4 KOSB suffered ten fatalities and another 65 wounded. German casualties during the dockyard fighting are unknown, though 5 KOSB claimed 400 POWs.

7th/9th Battalion, The Royal Scots, owed its fractional title to an amalgamation of two Territorial battalions. They were the last battalion of 155th Brigade to cross the Schelde, landing through knee-deep mud in the small hours of D+1. They spent the day flushing out snipers, rescuing Dutch civilians and patrolling FALMOUTH to pre-empt German attempts to infiltrate back into the beachhead from the Kernwerk. That night they moved centre stage to strike the final blow in the struggle for Vlissingen.

The last German stronghold remaining outside the docks was the luxurious pre-war Hotel Grand Britannia. Half a mile (800m) west of DOVER, up above the floods on Boulevard Evertsen, it was the nerve centre of the German defence: a minor fortress, surrounded by trenches, pillboxes and gun emplacements cunningly painted to look like house fronts, with a 2cm Flak Vierling on the roof. When Colonel Melvill (*sic*) received orders at

2130hrs on 2 November to assault the hotel the next morning, brigade minimized the difficulty of its capture. The garrison was only 50 strong, with no opposition expected along the way. Floodwater on the landward side was at most 2ft (1m) deep. A couple of rifle companies could do the job easily.

After studying town plans and aerial photographs, Melvill decided to take most of his battalion. Only A Company was left behind, searching warehouses in FALMOUTH. The plan was to attack from the north, as follows:

D Company on the right (Major Chater)
B Company on the left (Major Rose)
C Company in support to give covering fire (Captain Thomson)
Carrier Platoon (without vehicles) on flanks with extra PIATs and Bren guns.

As the approach was under water, three Weasels and some assault boats were taken for spare ammunition and casualty evacuation. Everyone wore Mae West lifebelts underneath the mountaineering smocks the battalion still wore.

The start line was Vrydom Weg, a pleasant tree-lined suburban road a couple of hundred yards (200–250m) from the back of the objective. To get there, the Royal Scots had to wade three-quarters of a mile (1.25km) from the crossroads at BEXHILL, along Badhuisstraat to the water tower at the junction with Koudekerksweg. Here they would bear half right between the hospital and Villa Park, an old cemetery, before turning left into Vrydom Weg. Two medium regiments would shell the objective from 0145 to 0210hrs, and four field regiments from 0245 to 0315hrs. German reports confirm, 'very heavy effective fire with phosphorous from 4–5 batteries in southern Zealand at 0200hrs, direct shelling of battle headquarters naval command Vlissingen'.

As the battalion advanced down Badhuisstraat by the light of burning houses at 0145hrs on 3 November, the water was over their knees, and soon got deeper. One Jock suggested perhaps they had landed in Venice by mistake. Order of march was: Carrier Platoon, B and D Companies, Tactical Headquarters and C Company. Hopes of an unopposed approach were disappointed as shellfire took out half the Carrier Platoon. The advance stalled while the FOO assembled his wireless and called for counterbattery fire. Then a hostile machine-gun post had to be evicted from the water tower. Progress against the 5-knot current, twice walking pace, was slow. The men advanced in file with linked arms, the taller ones interspersed with the short to keep the latter's heads above water. Somehow the wireless and PIAT operators contrived to hold their loads above water.

Near the start line, the leading files found themselves up to their necks, and the snake-like column doubled back to shallower waters near the Vredehof Laan junction. The order of attack was modified to allow for the change of direction:

B Company leading on the right (Major Rose)
D Company on the left in support (Major Chater)
C Company covering fire from the left (Captain Thomson)
Carrier Platoon covering fire from the right.

The first objective was a pillbox in Burgemeester van Woelderenlaan at the foot of the embankment, which D Company's No. 16 Platoon stormed noisily at 0415hrs, taking 30 prisoners. B and D Companies then closed up to the sandy embankment, perhaps 20ft high (6m). Today this is thick with vegetation, not evident in photographs taken at the time. Not all the sections made it, as they came under fire from flank and rear. Majors Rose and Chater made a quick plan for a composite platoon of D Company to rush the hotel, covered by fire from B Company and a platoon of C Company. Nos. 17 and 18 Platoons smashed down the doors, and broke into the ground floor, sealing off the basement. D Company's final platoon followed at 0600hrs, occupying the upper floor – standard house-clearing drill. Except for an officer shooting three German machine-gunners with his pistol, little certain is known about the mayhem that ensued for the next few hours in the hotel's smoke-filled corridors.

The senior officers left outside had no way of following what was happening, as German fire swept all approaches, frustrating any attempt to get in or out. The commanders of C and D Companies were both killed trying to join the troops in the building, while B Company was pinned down along the embankment by grenades, machine guns and 2cm cannon. The hotel was ablaze, ammunition dwindling, casualties mounting and wireless batteries running low. Had it been possible to call for artillery or air support, the two sides were too close together to do so safely. Driven out of his tactical headquarters by a German counterattack, Lt. Col. Melvill and his personal signaller were picked off by a sniper, the rifleman firing repeatedly to make sure.

About 0630hrs, C Company's No. 13 Platoon successfully reached the hotel, tasked with silencing the 2cm on the roof. Unable to find his way up inside the building, Lieutenant Beveridge climbed a drainpipe under fire, his appearance over the parapet so unnerving the gunners that they fled downstairs. Coincidentally, the battalion's only remaining field officer, Major Rose, organized a last dash at the outer defences. Encouraged by the silencing of the Flak Vierling, and enraged at the shooting of their colonel, B Company knocked out the remaining pillboxes along the embankment with PIATs, scaled the embankment, seized the trench along the top and stormed the 'White House' from where the colonel had been shot.

Meanwhile, within the burning hotel matters came to a head. As the labyrinthine corridors filled with smoke, the three platoon commanders inside agreed they should fight their way out along a concrete trench system to the south. Smashing down the entrance of the basement next door, they found a huge underground command shelter packed with Germans. Among them was Oberst Reinhardt of Grenadier-Regiment 1019, commanding the defence of

Vlissingen. With water all round, the enemy above and threatened with an explosive charge being thrown through the door, he surrendered. German wireless communications held up to the end. Reinhardt had reported the enemy breakthrough into the flooded zone near the water tower, the preparatory shellfire, and the start of close-quarters attacks at 0530hrs with tank support, an exaggerated view of the Weasel's combat value. He had expected Vlissingen's defenders to fight to the last man, and was shocked to be told that 600 POWs had been taken already.

The German naval wireless station finally packed up at 1100 or 1130 hrs, after receiving the Commanding Admiral's recognition of their courageous stand. Situation reports stressed that security had been preserved, the encryption machines being destroyed in good time. At 1200hrs, Marine-Flak-Abteilung 810's headquarters reported from the dunes overlooking Vlissingen to the north-west that large numbers of officers and soldiers had been seen leaving the hotel as prisoners. With the capture of Reinhardt and his naval colleague Würdemann, the battle for Vlissingen ended as a coherent entity, although Kernwerk held out until next day. Fifty Germans lay dead around the burnt-out hotel, and another 600 were captured. The Royal Scots' losses are often understated. The war diary gives three officers and 17 other ranks killed, with two more dying of wounds. The colonel and 52 other ranks were wounded. Major (later Colonel) Rose was awarded the Distinguished Service Order.

STORMING THE BATTERIES II: DISHOEK

West of Vlissingen, the British priority for D+1 was to capture the last remaining coastal battery: Marineküstenbatterie Dishoek or W11, manned by MAA 8/202 with four casemated 15cm guns. Its capture was assigned to Lieutenant-Colonel Farndale Phillips's 47 (RM) Commando, which had landed so uncomfortably the day before. By dawn 2 November, they had mostly reassembled south of the Westkapelle gap. A, Q and X Troops were intact, as was the Heavy Weapons Troop. Half of B Troop and some of Y were still missing.

47 (RM) Commando's assault on W11 resembled 48's attack on W13 the previous day, only more difficult. Both Commandos advanced rapidly, losing a troop to mortar fire soon after making contact with the enemy. Both had to wait while a fire plan was put together, attacking late in the short November afternoon. Both entered the enemy position, failing to clear it completely before nightfall. 48 (RM) Commando, however, had attacked an hour earlier, the extra daylight allowing air support and enough time to consolidate. 47 (RM) Commando attacked in gathering darkness, without air support. It failed to keep up with the supporting artillery fire and pulled back with heavy losses, including all five rifle troop commanders. A second attack was required next morning. Such was the confusion caused by the featureless dunes and intermingling of troops that Phillips doubted whether a complete and accurate account of the action could ever be written.

At dawn on D+1, 48 (RM) Commando found the Flak position south of W13 had been abandoned, and set off for Zouteland. A Troop entered the village at 1115hrs, capturing 150 prisoners after a short firefight. Just as the troop commander reassured the burgomaster the village was safe, a final 15in. shell from HMS *Erebus* crashed through the church roof, luckily without hurting anyone.

47 (RM) Commando passed through at 1248hrs, dumping their small packs south of the village. Mortars and machine guns were still struggling forwards. There was no transport, the Buffaloes held up by sand and stray mines. Everything had to be carried. The axis of advance followed the top of the dunes, 200–300 yards wide at this point (180–270m). Q and X Troops led on a two-troop front, accompanied by one Vickers gun, the other crew carrying ammunition. They advanced cautiously, moving by bounds from one crest to the next, one section always on the ground. Numerous prisoners came in, encouraged by an English-speaking POW.

As the dunes narrowed, Q Troop took the lead. About 1330hrs they reached the anti-tank obstacle at Groot Valkenisse. This was the north-western tip of Verteidigungsbereich Vlissingen: three rows of concrete dragon's teeth, laced with mines, running inland from the dunes to a 30ft-wide (25m) water-filled ditch. Resistance stiffened as a sniper shot an officer and sergeant. When the dunes widened out again beyond Groot Valkenisse, Q and X Troops took the seaward side, Y echeloned back on the crest, with A and B further behind. Six hundred yards (550m) further on, west of Klein Valkenisse, the lead sections came under fire from a strongpoint on the ridge to their left, known as Stützpunkt Carmen to the Germans, W238 to the British. The troop commander laid on smoke, and ordered 'right flanking'. There were bursts of machine-gun fire, and both troops came under heavy mortar fire. Eleven marines were killed outright; Q troop commander and 11 more wounded. Morale was badly shaken: some of X Troop who carried the wounded back to the Regimental Aid Post stopped there for the night; most of Q withdrew to the anti-tank obstacle without orders. A wounded sergeant rallied a few men, however, and gained a foothold on the ridge, the enemy retreating into W11.

W11 or Fidelio was a mile south of the anti-tank obstacle (1.6km), and about 1,000 yards (900m) from Carmen. It extended nearly half a mile (800m) along the dunes. The M170 casemates of its four main guns sat 85 yards (78m) apart just below the crest of the dunes in a ragged line. They were protected by a variety of supporting works, including two 2cm Flak, three type 612 artillery bunkers mounting plundered Belgian field guns, and a tangle of shelters, weapon pits, barbed wire and trenches. HMS *Erebus* conducted four shoots against the area during D+1, claiming 27 hits out of 99, two directly on a casemate. Bomber Command had previously dropped 385 500lb bombs on it, supplemented by over 2,000 7.2in. and 155mm shells on D-day. The battery reported one main gun silenced and its light anti-aircraft guns out of action. British investigators considered all the main guns

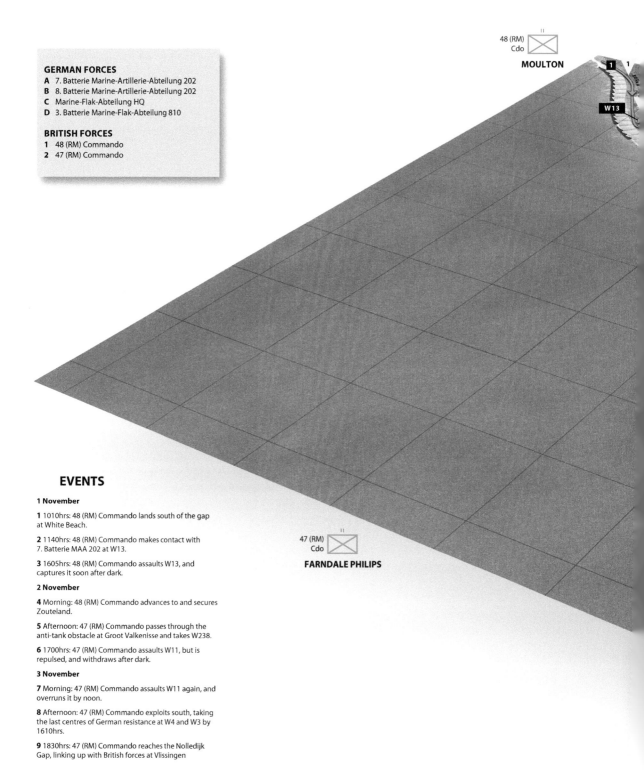

GERMAN FORCES
A 7. Batterie Marine-Artillerie-Abteilung 202
B 8. Batterie Marine-Artillerie-Abteilung 202
C Marine-Flak-Abteilung HQ
D 3. Batterie Marine-Flak-Abteilung 810

BRITISH FORCES
1 48 (RM) Commando
2 47 (RM) Commando

48 (RM)
Cdo
MOULTON

47 (RM)
Cdo
FARNDALE PHILIPS

EVENTS

1 November

1 1010hrs: 48 (RM) Commando lands south of the gap at White Beach.

2 1140hrs: 48 (RM) Commando makes contact with 7. Batterie MAA 202 at W13.

3 1605hrs: 48 (RM) Commando assaults W13, and captures it soon after dark.

2 November

4 Morning: 48 (RM) Commando advances to and secures Zouteland.

5 Afternoon: 47 (RM) Commando passes through the anti-tank obstacle at Groot Valkenisse and takes W238.

6 1700hrs: 47 (RM) Commando assaults W11, but is repulsed, and withdraws after dark.

3 November

7 Morning: 47 (RM) Commando assaults W11 again, and overruns it by noon.

8 Afternoon: 47 (RM) Commando exploits south, taking the last centres of German resistance at W4 and W3 by 1610hrs.

9 1830hrs: 47 (RM) Commando reaches the Nolledijk Gap, linking up with British forces at Vlissingen

ADVANCE THROUGH THE DUNES

The main objective of Operation *Infatuate* was to eliminate the batteries along Walcheren's south-west coast. The only land approach to these was along the sand dunes, on a narrow frontage between the sea and the flooded polderland on the left. 48 (RM) Commando led off on D-day, taking W13 by evening. W11 resisted 47 (RM) Commando's initial attack on D+1, but fell early next morning, followed by the final German positions at W4 and W3.

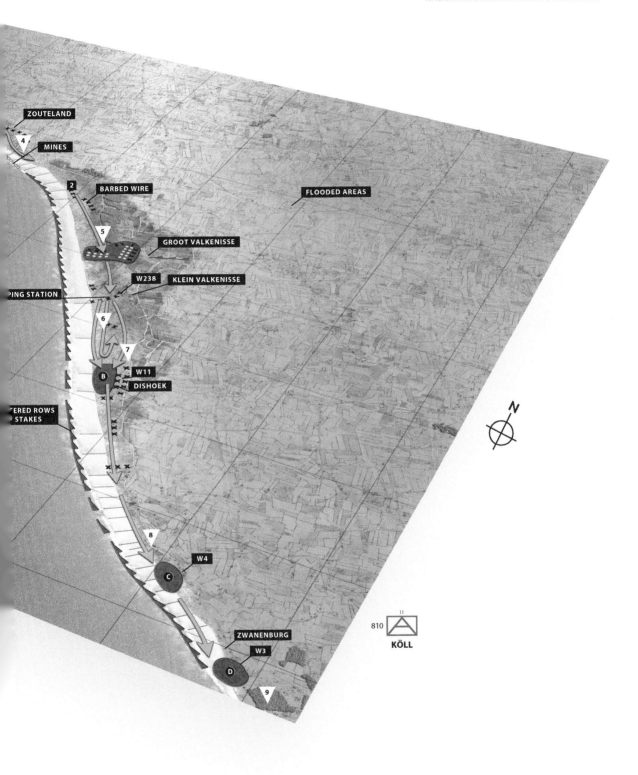

ZOUTELAND

4

MINES

2

BARBED WIRE

5

GROOT VALKENISSE

FLOODED AREAS

W238   KLEIN VALKENISSE

ING STATION

6

7

B   W11

DISHOEK

ERED ROWS
STAKES

8

W4

C

N

ZWANENBURG

W3

810   KÖLL

D

9

'self-destroyed', although 47's intelligence sergeant recalled one gun crew sitting round their gun, all killed by blast. The only certain hit was on the command post, destroying the battery range-finder.

Mid-afternoon of D+1, Lt. Col. Phillips was 1,000 yards (900m) short of his final objective. His difficulties resembled Moulton's the day before, only more so. Deteriorating weather had driven away the fighter-bombers he had seen earlier. Only one of his 3in. mortars was in touch, and that was slow into action. The base-plate position was poor and communications ineffective. There was plenty of artillery, however. Three medium regiments fired a series of concentrations, or 'stonks', straight along the top of the dunes ahead of the advancing commandos. The fire plan began at 1655hrs, five minutes before zero-hour, the concentrations lifting southwards every ten minutes, with a final three-regiment 'stonk' on the objective itself. Unfortunately the commandos had underestimated the delaying effects of enemy resistance and sand, and could not keep up with the barrage. Their failure to do so was fatal, allowing German snipers and machine-gunners to come back into action before they could be overrun.

Y Troop crossed the start line at 1700hrs, sections leapfrogging forwards covered by smoke from their 2in. mortars. Passing Q Troop's casualties, they suffered further losses from enemy artillery and the sections coalesced as everyone dashed forwards to seek cover in dead ground. When they checked, A Troop passed through, nearly reaching the 'umbrella feature', by which Phillips seems to have meant the type 120 command bunker at W11's northern end, with its concrete roof elevated above the observation platform. Germans were soon surrendering to A Troop, who left them to B Troop mopping up behind. Y Troop came forwards, and the intermingled commandos worked round either flank, instinctively following their battle drill in the gathering darkness. Both groups made progress, one getting behind the first gun casemate before machine-gun fire and stick grenades knocked out the senior troop officers and brought the advance to a stop. X Troop attacked 20–30 minutes after the leading troops, but never reached the final objective.

It was now quite dark. Realizing they had shot their bolt, the junior officers and NCOs still on their feet extracted their wounded, and withdrew through a series of layback positions. Eventually they met X Troop with the adjutant and second-in-command, stopping about 500 yards back (450m), near a searchlight platform, to seaward of the dunes. Here they were counterattacked by 15 Germans, who cheekily called on them to surrender. Timings agree with Kriegsmarine claims that at 1730hrs the Dishoek battery and 3/810 (West Vlissingen) were resisting enemy attacks from the north-west with their remaining guns, and that the enemy penetrating W11 were driven out about 1800hrs, following a counterattack by naval troops. The German command, however, doubted W11's chances of holding out against superior enemy forces.

Phillips was equally pessimistic about renewing the attack that night. He had no reserve, Q Troop had disintegrated and until 2100hrs he had no clear idea where his other troops were. He resolved to wait for daylight, while the mortars and machine guns were brought up, the wounded evacuated and a POW cage established. At 0100hrs on D+2 Brigadier Leicester arrived at Phillips's tactical headquarters, now at the searchlight platform, with the fire-eating Moulton. They pressed Phillips to put in a night attack, but he declined. Leicester let the matter drop, even Moulton admitting later that events proved him right. A more entertaining diversion was provided by two self-styled

W11 photographed from the sea in the late 1940s. The commandos advanced from left to right, X and A Troops storming uphill into the centre of the battery, under covering fire from B Troop on the leftmost casemate roof. (Photo © Hans Sakkers)

'nurses', who wandered into British lines wearing crudely stencilled Red Crosses on their frocks, but had hysterics when confronted with casualties.

Next morning, 3 November, surviving troop officers counted heads, while Phillips inspected the German position, and made a new plan.

B Troop was to lead the main attack along the dunes, reinforced by the Intelligence Section and a Dutch section from No. 10 Commando, and followed by A Troop. X Troop was to give covering fire while Q and Y Troops with one Vickers gun were positioned on the left flank to prevent enemy crossfire from inland, which had caused problems the evening before. A Troop of 48 (RM) Commando (unacknowledged in Phillips's account) were to push even further to the left front, to provide enfilading fire from a pumping station on the edge of the floods. The mortars were to support the attack from near the anti-tank obstacle, first with smoke and then high explosive. Artillery support was to consist of 'Mike targets', regimental concentrations put down every two or three hundred yards down the dunes in front of the advancing commandos – another medium regiment to put down harassing fire about 1,000 yards (900m) beyond the Commando's immediate objective. Stormy weather precluded air support.

Nobody remembered afterwards whether H-hour was at 0830 or 0900hrs, but supporting fire from mortars and flanking parties was effective, communications worked well and everything went to plan. B and A Troops worked their way along the seaward side of the dunes towards the first casemate, under increasingly heavy fire. A Troop got past the bunker, but was held up by grenades, until B Troop caught up. At first they lined the grass bank around the well in which the bunker stood. Then they climbed onto its roof to cut away the surrounding wire. Meanwhile, the colonel had ordered X Troop forwards along the beach to assault the position from that direction, preceded by the adjutant.

The latter then led X and A Troops (left and right flank respectively) uphill into the centre of the battery, while B Troop provided covering fire from the first casemate roof. Q and Y Troops having cleared the accommodation bunkers to landward, reached the top of the dunes behind the battery about the same time, bringing the Germans within W11 under attack from three sides. As soon as X and A Troops got into the battery, the defenders began to surrender in large numbers, many glassy-eyed and speechless from the bombardment. The Royal Navy had gambled on their guns being beyond use. At 1230hrs, according to MFA 810, four British minesweepers were already at work in the Wielingen Channel.

The W11 area today, from the southern end of the battery, looking back along the dunes towards Zouteland in the far distance, the direction of 47 (RM) Commando's advance. (Photo © Richard Brooks)

Philips now exploited forwards along the dunes, sending B Troop right, A Troop left, with X Troop in the low ground inland on the left. Q and Y Troops followed to mop up, accompanied by 48's lone troop. Three prisoners went along to summon their countrymen to surrender, which they did in embarrassing numbers. Other POWs helped by carrying forward 3in. mortar ammunition, although there was no chance to use this. Abandoning tactical precautions, 47 (RM) Commando swept down the dunes to the last German positions on their side of the Nolledijk Gap: MFA 810's headquarters at W4, and Marineflakbatterie West (3/810) at W3.

These should have been tough nuts to crack, containing 200–300 troops with three 75mm guns and a mine-infested anti-tank ditch. The Kriegsmarine reported the commander of MFA 810 and his men stood ready for the attack, while sending in a stream of reports about traffic over the Schelde, fighting in Vlissingen, destruction of all secret material, and so on. The British reached W4 about midday, but were driven off again at 1334hrs. The wireless reported, 'Fighting against overwhelming force. In good shape', then nothing more was heard. 'Thus', crowed the Kriegsmarine, 'the struggle here was also one of heroic resistance to the end.'

Reality was less dramatic. The commandos arrived about 1530hrs, B Troop up on the dunes, A Troop on the low ground astride the road. One unlucky Marine was shot dead in a last flurry of small-arms fire. A German officer proposed a truce to pick up the wounded. Phillips refused, threatening a two-Commando assault with air and artillery support, an inspired bluff. By 1610hrs, all resistance had ceased with the surrender of 200 Germans, including Korvettenkapitän Köll, who invited a confused Phillips to shoot him if he had not done his duty. By 1830hrs the British had reached the Nolledijk Gap, the commandos on either side able to pick out the green berets beyond. The Walcheren assault's main objective had been achieved

BRIDGEHEAD LOGISTICS

The success of amphibious landings depends as much on overcoming difficulties of supply as defeating the enemy. The physical separation of the two Walcheren landings doubled the logistical risks, as both beachheads had to be nourished until ground troops could link them up. The rapid progress on either side of the Nolledijk Gap, however, gave the British a choice of supply lines, should enemy action or the weather deny them use of either beachhead.

Vlissingen's Uncle Beach had fewer apparent advantages than Westkapelle's Green Beach, but it proved the better bet. Congested at high tide, Uncle Beach was 2ft (1m) deep in slimy mud at low water, hampering the unloading of stores. Uncomfortably close to the front line, it suffered from snipers, although these desisted when captured Germans joined in the beach work. Some of the latter were remarkably willing to help, a commando joking that they did far more for the Allies than they ever had for the Third Reich. Uncle Beach had two particular advantages: the LCOCU and sappers quickly cleared it of obstacles, while its sheltered location inside the Schelde protected it from the worst effects of the onshore winds. Stormy weather briefly interrupted the LVT ferry service from Breskens on D+2, but the Vlissingen beachhead never experienced the same logistical difficulties as Westkapelle.

Operations on Green Beach faced a challenging combination of enemy countermeasures, both active and passive, and physical handicaps, both topographical and meteorological. These were compounded by a muddle on landing. Three of the Royal Engineer's four LCTs touched down north of the gap instead of south, with four out of the five bulldozers driving straight into a patch of mud. One, D7, did land south of the gap, but fell into a submerged crater before reaching firm ground, and it drowned. In addition, only one of the RE's five LVTs made it ashore intact. Personnel mostly landed safely, but without the heavy equipment needed for clearing and maintaining the beachhead. Meanwhile naval beach and signals parties on Green Beach attracted accurate mortar and artillery fire. The beach sign put up to guide incoming landing craft was soon shot away, although enemy fire slackened once 41 (RM) Commando captured the Westkapelle lighthouse.

The Beach Maintenance Area at Green beach, exposed to W11's indirect fire and westerly gales that blew up on D+2, the Westkapelle BMA was less than satisfactory. Three LCTs were lost unloading stores before it closed down on D+8. (Photo © Richard Brooks)

Sand dunes defiladed Green Beach from W11, but enemy observers could still see approaching landing craft, and knew where they must come ashore. Every attempt to land supplies or evacuate casualties on D-day was frustrated by shellfire. Of the three LCTs loaded with stores, one was sunk en route by a mine, and the other two ordered off after one was hit by shellfire. Another LCT was driven off during the afternoon. Not until darkness fell did an LCT beach successfully to take off 150 casualties and a large number of captured Germans. In the absence of barbed wire, the POW 'cage' consisted of a large bomb crater, but the defeated enemy were conveniently docile.

The engineers' first task was to clear a level space for the Beach Maintenance Area (BMA) and Field Dressing Station, just north of the radar station. The only practical site was pitted with bomb craters and full of mines. Weasels crossed these safely enough, but the LVTs suffered heavily. Many were lost, the worst incident involving a Buffalo full of wounded commandos, six of whom burned to death. A mine-free lane was cleared using prodders and mine detectors, but passing vehicles continually turned up fresh mines, making it necessary to resweep the lane every two hours. Surgical units remained in their LVTs, as it was too dangerous outside for them to operate. Luckily there were few abdominal wounds requiring major surgery, most of the casualties being to mines and mortar fragments.

W11 remained a threat throughout D+1, plastering the beach at 0400hrs with star shells and high explosive. When the two surviving stores LCTs approached the beach at 1330hrs with a casualty evacuation LCI(S), the battery once more opened fire. One LCT was straddled, and all three craft withdrew. Several LVTs were hit, their ammunition and petrol exploding for several hours, while the prisoners sang 'Deutschland Über Alles'.

The beachmaster decided to open a new beach, but the obstacles behind demanded a bulldozer. The LCOCU tried blowing them up, but it was slow, dangerous work that left jagged steel projecting from the sand. At low tide the last bulldozer waded across from Westkapelle, to loud cheers, as water lapped the driving compartment windows. It promptly ploughed up the offending obstacles, and cut a road through the dunes, allowing LVTs to bypass the minefield. It then began filling in the worst craters, falling in twice. Rescued by prisoners of war, it was finally immobilized when it lost a track to a mine. Late on D+1, W11 was distracted by the approach of 47 (RM) Commando. Its final shell fell on the BMA about 1700hrs, although nobody yet knew that it was the last.

As the battle moved away from the BMA, supplies had to be moved up to the advanced troops. The road south was all under water, except the final stretch into Zouteland. Winding between craters and minefields, LVTs beat a crazy path along the foot of the dunes, on which they later continued to Vlissingen. The going was so bad that the 4km (2½ miles) to Zouteland took over half an hour, and was impossible at night. An edgy Lt. Col. Phillips accused his LVT officer of compromising the attack on W11 for want of mortar bombs. Improving the route without heavy plant was slow, hard work, LVT tracks being peculiarly destructive of any made-up surface. Once W11 had fallen, most of the LVTs went north to support operations beyond Westkapelle. There was a reasonable brick road through Domburg, between the craters, but crossing the gap remained an unpleasant job. Seas ran high, and it was never safe for Weasels.

Once W11 was silenced, 8 Canadian FSU could open its surgical set and begin to operate on the most urgent cases. The two stores LCTs finally beached a day and a half late at 0300hrs on D+2. Unloading began at once, but, despite help from POWs, neither had finished before high water that afternoon when the weather altered for the worse. One of the LCTs broached to and was lost. The other had made fast to a groyne and German beach obstructions, and continued unloading through D+3. By then a shuttle service from Ostend should have been in place to bring supplies in and take casualties out, but the weather continued to deteriorate. Landing craft approaching the beach were turned away, and eventually driven back to Ostend by the storm. On D+4 the last stores LCT carried away her stern lines, crashed into the groyne and filled with water. An anxious brigade headquarters requested a supply airdrop, although the troops were happy enough eating captured German rations.

The gales moderated sufficiently on D+5 (6 November) for an LCI(S) to take off walking wounded, but yet another LCT loaded with stores dragged her anchor, becoming a total loss. Two more LCTs landed Weasels and extra bulldozers, and took off more casualties, POWs and other passengers. Green Beach was then closed down, as the less hazardous Vlissingen route became the main line of communication. The LVTs remained until 4th SS Brigade left the island, regrouping back at Terneuzen on 14 November. They were as indispensable in the flooded hinterland as on the coast, and were overworked accordingly. Of the 104 that left Ostend on 31 October, 27 were written off, and the others rendered unfit for service.

THE SURRENDER OF MIDDELBURG

When Operation *Infatuate* began, 2nd Canadian Infantry Division was already knocking on Walcheren's back door: the causeway across the Sloe Channel, between Goes on South Beveland and Arnemuiden on Walcheren. It was an uninviting venue for an offensive. Half a mile long (800m), not 100 yards wide (90m), dead straight and completely open, it featured a badly cratered brick road, three or four feet (1m) above the neighbouring mudflats, a single-track railway, a bicycle path and a line of telegraph poles. At high tide, the mudflats on either side provided insufficient water for an assault boat, while at low water they were too soft even for infantry. Even Weasels with their low ground pressure could not negotiate the numerous runnels that intersected the flats. Machine guns and at least one 88mm anti-tank gun swept the causeway end to end, and Artillerie-Regiment 170 at Arnemuiden and Nieuwland was well in range.

Three successive battalions of 5th Canadian Infantry Brigade battled to establish a bridgehead between 31 October and 2 November. Armoured vehicles could not cross in face of solid 88mm shot ricocheting down the causeway, leaving the infantry to face the music alone. By 2 November, D+1 at Westkapelle, le Régiment de Maisonneuve had carved out a small fire-swept bridgehead west of the causeway. 1st Glasgow Highlanders relieved them later that day, as 52nd (Lowland) Division took over operations in Walcheren. The Canadians were pulled out for a well-deserved rest. Since 29 September, when it advanced from Antwerp to cut Walcheren off, 2nd Canadian Infantry Division had taken over 5,200 prisoners, and suffered 3,650 casualties.

Most of Hakewill-Smith's division was now in South Beveland, although he himself remained at Hulst south of the Schelde to oversee operations at Vlissingen. Hakewill-Smith had no time for the Canadians' head-on approach to the causeway. When Simond's stand-in at II Canadian Corps demanded another frontal assault, he said it was not a viable military operation and threatened to protest to 21st Army Group. Threatened with the sack, he gained 48 hours to find another way round.

Hakewill-Smith had already ordered a set of enlarged aerial photographs of the Sloe Channel. As soon as his divisional engineers looked at these, they saw the way across, 'crystal clear'. On the night of 1–2 November, two Royal

Aerial view of the Markt or market place at Middelburg. Walcheren's largest town suffered little damage during the liberation, the German surrender pre-empting the heavy bombardments suffered by Vlissingen and Westkapelle. (Photo © Richard Brooks)

Engineers crawled along the watershed, following bearings and distances surveyed that afternoon, until they heard German voices, and crawled back. The crossing place was about 2 miles (3km) south of the causeway, between the villages of Nieuwdorp and Oudedorp, either side of the Sloe, at the northern end of the Channel's sea branch. It was an unlikely line of attack from the German perspective. A number of their men had drowned there in 1940, and the British took care not to betray their intentions.

Since the war, the area has been reclaimed, the mudflats replaced by the Vlissingen-Oost industrial zone. The successive objectives of the attack, however, can still be followed from the roughly parallel roads that lay between the Sloe and the village of Nieuw-en-Sint Joosland (usually abbreviated to Nieuwland), about half a mile apart (800m). These were codenamed after horse-racing events, as follows:

DERBY: the old sea dyke, between the polder and the Sloe (now underneath the industrial zone);
LEGER: Binnendijk (Inner dyke), and EPSOM a little further north on the same road;
OAKS: Boomdijk, south of Nieuwland;
YORK: Langeweg, north of Nieuwland.

The crossing itself was appropriately codenamed Operation *Mallard*. The plan was for the RE reconnaissance party to return next night, 2–3 November, mark the route with white tape, and lead across 6th Cameronians, temporarily under command of 157th Brigade. It would be a silent crossing in assault boats, A and B Companies leading, to seize DERBY Right and Left respectively, followed by battalion headquarters and the regimental aid post. C and D Companies would then pass through to LEGER.

The engineers were delayed by the difficult terrain, the main crossing not starting until 0330hrs. Ten minutes paddling brought the Cameronians to the salt marshes beyond the tidal channel. Then they faced a gruelling hour-long slog through thick clinging mud, knee or waist deep, to the sea-dyke. The lead companies took their objectives with little trouble, C Company passing through to LEGER Right at 0700hrs. D Company on the left was less fortunate, meeting determined opposition as they passed through DERBY. Overwhelmed by artillery and small-arms fire from their open left flank, none of the platoons reached their objective at LEGER Left, the Land-en-Zeezicht crossroad, now opposite the N254 motorway's 26km marker. B Company tried to restart the attack, but both companies were pinned down by a hail of fire from mortars, high-velocity guns, machine guns and snipers. By noon D Company had suffered heavy losses, including the company commander killed. The survivors pulled back to the beach, no longer an effective fighting unit. B Company withdrew to DERBY Left, still under artillery and mortar fire, but sheltered from the enfilading small arms. The RAP was packed with casualties, who could not be evacuated through the curtain of German shells falling on the only crossing place. Wireless communications were 'disconnected', and the battalion led by the second-in-command, as the colonel was still east of the Sloe. Weasels stuck in the salt marsh or were hit by shellfire. Very little food or ammunition got through to the battalion. At dusk a few reinforcements arrived from 5th Battalion Highland Light Infantry, but choppy seas, whipped up by the high winds that did so much damage at Green Beach, put a stop to boating. The beachhead was isolated.

Operation *Mallard*: crossing the Sloe, 3 November

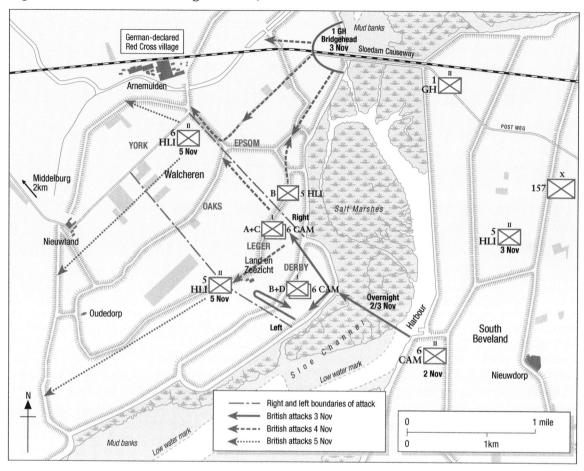

Despite these difficulties, the crossing reduced the pressure on the Glasgow Highlanders almost immediately. An early-morning German counterattack on the bridgehead ended with 85 of the attackers surrendering, and prisoners continued to come in all day, despite the 'friendly' machine-gun fire directed at them. At 1100hrs the mortar platoon engaged and drove off a rare German self-propelled gun. Typhoon fighter-bombers made the most of the sunshine to launch repeated strikes on German positions. By evening, 294 Germans had surrendered. Fighting patrols went out to occupy their empty positions, ending the day within half a mile of the Cameronians' right flank at EPSOM.

Next day, 4 November, the weight of the British attack began to tell, as their massively superior artillery and Typhoons eroded German morale and indirect fire capability. Across the still choppy Sloe Channel, a new '22' set restored communications with the Cameronians by midday, and 5 HLI crossed soon after, accompanied by 4.2in. mortars from A Company, 7 Manchesters. The two effective Cameronian companies then put in a couple of divergent attacks to clear their front; A Company pushed forward to the Groenenburg crossroads at OAKS, taking prisoners as they went, while C Company struck half left to take LEGER Left. By last light, the Cameronians held OAKS Right and Left, and the HLI had come through on either flank to link up with the Glasgow Highlanders at EPSOM, and relieve the

Cameronians' B Company at DERBY and LEGER Left. The eastern bridgehead was now 2 miles (3km) across and 2,000 yards (2km) deep, leaving the Germans no realistic hope of containing it.

The following day, the Lowlanders kept up the pressure, pouring fresh battalions into the dry corner of the island. 5 HLI drove south-west to Fort Ramekens, whose commandant surrendered when threatened with five medium and four field regiments. On the right, 6 HLI advanced to Nieuwland, 2 miles (3km) from Middelburg across the floods. The Glasgow Highlanders provided a firm base, and picketed Arnemuiden, which the Germans had declared an open town, a *Lazarettdorf* or hospital village. Resistance was crumbling and many prisoners captured. The Glasgow Highlanders' score for the day was 355. All three field regiments advanced, through atrocious going, to firing positions south-east of Arnemuiden, covering Middelburg, while light anti-aircraft guns protected the causeway itself. 156th Brigade attacked north from the causeway, advancing to Kleverskerke on the Veere Canal. 7 Cameronians took 1,200 prisoners, 'without close fighting', the Germans surrendering when mortared or on first sight of troops advancing. Wehrmacht POWs blamed Kriegsmarine diehards for prolonging the defence of Veere. They had noticed their commanders' tendency to evacuate 'key' personnel, leaving the soldiers to do their best. Food was short, as was fighting spirit. Seekommandant Vlissingen noted, as he himself left for Schouwen, that Veere's garrison was looting tinned food, while naval gun crews had to be kept at their posts by infantrymen.

Middelburg was now in a critical state. The Germans' outer defences had all fallen, from the Sloe right round to Westkapelle, past Vlissingen. Thousands of troops and Dutch civilians had taken refuge in the town. Food and water were in short supply. It was rumoured that Gen.Lt. Daser, Festungskommandant Walcheren, would surrender to tanks, like other German fortress commanders, but there seemed no way of satisfying this requirement. Direct access along the canal bank from Vlissingen was blocked by a pocket of resistance halfway between Souburg and Middelburg. Patrols from both KOSB battalions exchanged fire with this on 4–5 November, but

German POWs massed in the Damplein under the guns of a line of LVTs on the far side of the square. The Dutch policeman in the centre foreground seems more concerned with his excited compatriots than the prisoners. (Author's collection)

the rising tide covered the mine-strewn towpath. All ranks were feeling the strain of fighting up to their waist in cold water for days on end.

The problem was resolved by the Buffaloes of 11 RTR. These could cross floods, and looked quite like tanks. While the KOSBs probed along the canal, a lonely LVT charted a roundabout course from Vlissingen, to approach Middelburg via Koudekerke from the west. The reconnaissance party found the route both practicable and undefended. Next day, 6 November, the 11 LVTs in working order embarked A Company 7/9 Royal Scots, commanded by Major R. H. B. Johnston, some engineers and a machine-gun platoon from 7 Manchesters. Their orders were to reconnoitre in force, and if possible parley with the Germans. Just after noon, this tiny force set off across the flooded airfield north-west of Vlissingen, dodging the booby traps and wire. Cheering Dutch civilians waved them on their way, while protective Typhoons flew overhead. One LVT was left behind, entangled in the wire draped across the airfield. Another hit a mine near Torenvliedt, south-west of Middelburg, losing six men killed and six wounded. A third LVT went back to Vlissingen with the casualties incurred reconnoitring a German pillbox.

The remaining eight LVTs approached Middelburg towards 1630hrs, apparently unnoticed. Perhaps the garrison was distracted by Operation *Mallard*; perhaps they felt secure behind their moat. The place seemed deserted until the leading LVT turned a corner, and climbed up to a dry street to be greeted by ecstatic crowds of Dutch people. Shortly afterwards 6 HLI to the east reported 'loud cheering in Middelburg', and an all-clear siren was heard in the town. The column reached the main square before meeting any Germans, orderly crowds of whom appeared as the Royal Scots took up commanding positions around the square. The enemy clearly believed a large British force was loose in the town, and were delighted to be taken prisoner.

A number of Norwegian officers had been attached to 52nd Division, against its planned deployment to Norway. One had accompanied A Company as a German interpreter, so Johnston sent him off to Daser's headquarters in another square, the Damplein, to persuade the general to surrender. Daser's staff made no difficulties, but the old man was unwilling to capitulate to a mere lieutenant. By now the Damplein was rapidly filling up with field grey. Johnston thought some accelerated promotion was appropriate, and represented himself as a 'staff colonel', allegedly borrowing the necessary extra pips from a nearby subaltern. Threatened with the wholesale destruction of Middelburg by bombing, Daser scowled and gave in.

The situation remained tense as hundreds of Germans marched up, far outnumbering their captors. A staff officer who saw through the bluff was hastily locked away, but many of the troops outside were still armed. As rain began to fall, their mood soured. Any accidental collision with the enthusiastic Dutch crowds might precipitate a massacre. Fortunately the Resistance took a hand. Equipped with orange armbands and German rifles, they rounded up their own drunks, posted guards on the prisoners and mobilized the town's bakers to make bread for the dyspeptic multitude. Johnston's own brigade at Vlissingen could do little to help before morning, but about 0300hrs on 7 November, 5 HLI marched to the rescue, singing 'Lili Marlene'. At 0330hrs Johnston handed Middelburg over to their colonel, though he kept Daser, the first general the battalion had captured. Over 2,000 prisoners were taken, for no British casualties beyond those in the injured Buffaloes. The only formed body of Germans now left on Walcheren were the remains of Grenadier-Regiment 1020 beyond Domburg, with batteries W18 and W19.

LAST STAND IN THE NORTH

The elimination of German forces from Walcheren's north-west coast had to await reduction of the south-western batteries that prevented Allied shipping from entering the Westerschelde. Until that was done, 10 Commando, reinforced by two troops from 41 (RM) Commando, occupied a blocking position at Domburg to prevent any interference from that direction. The rest of 41 (RM) Commando crossed the Westkapelle gap on D+1 to support the other Royal Marine Commandos' advance towards Vlissingen. With the fall of W4, 41 (RM) Commando returned north. 4 and 48 (RM) Commandos followed, as the brigade tightened its grip upon Grenadier-Regiment 1020 and other German fragments holding out around Oostkapelle in hopes of escaping north across the Oosterschelde to Schouwen. They had little chance of this. The Kriegsmarine had specific orders to turn away would-be refugees from the Wehrmacht, if necessary by force.

Domburg remained under sniper and machine-gun fire throughout 2 November, until two Shermans and two AVREs arrived towards evening. These were the only four tanks still in action. Overnight the rising tide had drowned the other three AFVs (all Flails) to reach Westkapelle. Emboldened by the armour, 10 Commando requested permission to proceed northwards on the 3rd, but were told, 'Not at present'. The bombardment squadron had withdrawn, no support craft were available and the artillery at Breskens was reaching the limits of its range. Despite this, the Norwegians unofficially pushed forwards 1 mile (1.6km) into the Hoogduin, or high dunes, beyond Domburg, while the Belgians routed snipers out of the woods to the south. By evening, they had taken 211 prisoners, for the loss of one man killed and four wounded. As 48 (RM) Commando found at W13, the Kriegsmarine did not like close fighting.

41 (RM) Commando returned to Domburg on 4 November, in time to participate in another attack by 10 Commando, supported by tanks and artillery at 1500hrs. Enfiladed by heavy machine-gun fire from woods on the right flank, B Troop was unable to advance, and withdrew to consolidate

Walcheren falls: the British follow-up, 3–8 November

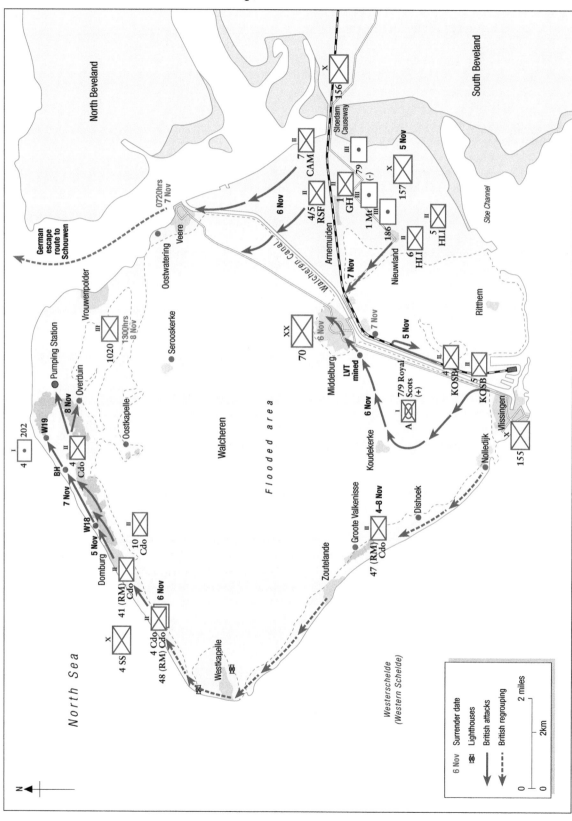

ground already taken. Nevertheless, the Belgians gained about 800 yards (750m) to the south of W18, the next major objective. The following day, 5 November, W18 was assaulted by 41 (RM) Commando on the left and the Norwegians on the right. Conditions were unfavourable for air support, delaying the attack until the afternoon. The Norwegians advanced through the woods at 1430hrs, A Troop moving forward at 1500hrs right of the dunes, and Y Troop on the left 15 minutes later, the armour providing the only direct fire support. Mines made for slow progress, one blowing the track off an AVRE, which had to be left, while machine-gunners in the woods enfiladed movement along the dunes. Two Nebelwerfer north of Oostkapelle gave trouble from a sinister location christened 'Black Hut' after its most conspicuous feature. Nevertheless, the attack went much according to plan, one of the Shermans blowing up the Nebelwerfer's rocket supply. A and Y Troops successfully assaulted the position, 41 (RM) Commando's second-in-command bringing forward P Troop to help consolidate after the Y Troop commander was killed. W18 was secured by 1615hrs, with about 300 prisoners, although enemy mortaring continued into the night.

It was not possible to follow up this success immediately. Minefields hindered resupply, and snipers infested the woods through which 10 Commando had to advance. By midnight 6 November, however, the Belgian Troop had skilfully made its way forward to gain the next day's start line ahead of time, while 4 and 48 (RM) Commandos had arrived at Domburg with brigade headquarters. The tanks moved into W18 and shot up various bunkers towards Black Hut, putting two rounds into the firing slit of a large concrete emplacement there at 2,000 yards (1,800m). Typhoons struck W19 with rockets, hitting guns and pillboxes, starting a large fire and blowing up an ammunition dump.

Black Hut was dealt with next day, 7 November. Typhoons strafed the area with rockets and 20mm cannon, while Shermans and the brigade's combined mortars gave close support. Black Hut was captured by 1400hrs, but the last AVRE ran over a large explosive device, killing three of the crew. The Sherman crews found two demolished Nebelwerfer and a 5cm anti-tank gun in the big emplacement, the marks of two high-explosive rounds on the inside rear wall, and 'plenty of blood on the floor'. Further rocket strikes on W19 took place that afternoon.

41 (RM) Commando pushed ahead without fire support; communications with the mortars had broken down, and heavy artillery was not allowed within 1,000 yards (900m) of the precious Oranjebosch pumping station

LEFT
3in. mortar, probably from 41 (RM) Commando, in action near Domberg. Mortars made an important contribution to the commandos' final advance, as they moved beyond the range of Allied artillery south of the Schelde. (Photo © Trustees of the Royal Marines Museum)

RIGHT
The last Sherman remaining at Westkapelle makes a fitting memorial to Walcheren's liberators. The inscription's final words read: 'Walcheren kan herrijsen' – 'Walcheren can rise again'. (Photo © Richard Brooks)

which supplied Middelburg's drinking water. Some 400 yards (350m) further along the dunes, A Troop tried to pass through B Troop, but ran into a minefield. While they were seeking a way round, heavy and accurate mortar fire came down, causing 12 casualties, one of whom died at once. The commanding officer decided to withdraw to Black Hut, and continue the advance when support was available.

For 8 November, or D+7, a brigade attack was planned with support from 52nd Division's 25-pdrs, now established east of Middelburg. Overnight artillery concentrations softened up suspected centres of resistance, especially in woods. The commandos pushed forwards under cover of darkness, as they had done in Vlissingen, dislocating the isolated and exhausted defenders. The two Shermans occupied a commanding position to shoot in the commandos, but all these elaborate preparations came to nothing. At 0830hrs 4 Commando, which had taken over the lead from 41 (RM) Commando, requested a ceasefire. Four well-armed Germans had been found in the Overduin woods outside Vrouwenpolder, saying they wished to discuss surrender terms. Lieutenant-Colonel Dawson spoke with Oberst Veigele over the field telephone in the Germans' command post, and then drove into Vrouwenpolder in a German staff car, his intelligence officer sitting on the bonnet. After an exchange of military compliments all German troops remaining in Walcheren laid down their arms, bringing the final number of prisoners captured by the brigade to approximately 2,900. This ended organized resistance on Walcheren, as Veere had capitulated to 7 Cameronians the previous morning. W19 surrendered with the rest, the Royal Engineers blowing up its five 3.7in. guns.

The handful of tanks present during the final advance had played a role out of all proportion to the number of vehicles. All the close support during this period came from Typhoons and tanks, the AVREs beating down a path for the less agile Shermans with their 75mm guns. Not only was the going very bad, with the ever-present threat of mines, there was no such thing as a hull-down position, the tanks having to skyline themselves to open fire. Between 3 and 8 November, they fired over 1,400 rounds of 75mm and 30 boxes of Browning machine-gun ammunition, while the AVREs fired 46 boxes of BESA. Prisoners emphasized the paralysing moral and material effect of the tanks, to which they had no answer. Conversely, the tanks greatly heartened the commandos, who had lost much of their equipment on landing, and until the final night lacked accurate close support from field artillery. Brigadier Leicester wrote that the handful of tanks had been worth their weight in gold. Driven back to Westkapelle, the two Shermans were stripped, and abandoned to the looting of the populace. Every armoured vehicle belonging to the armoured assault teams had been written off, but their effect had been decisive.

AFTER THE BATTLE

Lieutenant-General Simonds hailed the capture of Walcheren as 'a great and decisive victory'. Compared with major World War II battles, such as Stalingrad or Alamein, it involved few combatants and relatively limited loss of life. But its consequences were immense.

Precise figures for Allied losses are not easy to calculate. Casualty returns for the many individual units engaged are scattered throughout the official records. The table below summarizes the unit level figures that Paul Crucq has collated for 3 October through 8 November at formation level. Attached engineer units are included with their infantry, who suffered the majority of casualties once ashore:

Formation	Killed	Missing	Wounded	Total
RAF Bomber Command and 84 Group	55	–	–	55
Royal Navy	185	–	168	353+
52nd Division	96	–	297	393*
5th Canadian Brigade	34	2	100	136
4th Special Service Brigade	86	9	283	378
79th Armoured Division	25	1	45	71
Supporting RA, RE, Pioneers, RCAMC	8	47	32	87
TOTAL	489	59	925	1,473

(+) Omits casualties for LCA crews
(*) Includes divisional artillery, mostly from 452 Mountain Battery: three killed and nine wounded

About half the Allied losses occurred during Operation *Infatuate II*. A contemporary calculation put military casualties there at 468 out of 3,082 soldiers and marines committed, and naval losses at 350 out of 1,785 sailors and marines, mostly in the SSEF. On top of the British casualties were losses suffered by the Dutch population. Material losses were heavy in percentage terms: all 24 vehicles landed with the armoured assault teams were lost, with unknown quantities of amphibians; 17 out of 27 support craft were destroyed or rendered unfit for further action, as were 18 out of 35 LCTs and 42 out of 72 LCAs.

In return, 70. Infanterie-Division was written off completely, along with the capital cost of over 300 bunkers with their associated equipment and obstacles. German dead were uncounted, but perhaps not very numerous.

They fought behind fixed defences, and usually surrendered before it came to close-quarters fighting. At least 10,000 were taken prisoner, more than some previous estimates of the total defenders. The most disastrous loss for the Germans, however, was the opening of the Schelde. This was not a foregone conclusion. The Kriegsmarine had laid 1,703 ground and contact mines around the mouth of the Schelde, supplemented in September and October 1944 by 653 more within the estuary or covering Vlissingen. These had to be cleared before Allied merchant ships could reach Antwerp. Once the Walcheren batteries were silenced, however, the minefields provided a demonstration of the futility of obstacles that are not covered by fire.

Even before the batteries fell silent, Admiral Ramsay began preparations for a major minesweeping effort, codenamed Operation *Calendar*. Such was the urgency, the first ships set out for Breskens on D+1, returning to Ostend after they came under heavy fire. Next morning, 13 sweepers slipped safely past the batteries under cover of darkness. Operation *Calendar* began on 4 November or D+3. Force 'A' from Sheerness swept up to Terneuzen, dealing with 50 mines. Six of the Breskens sweepers proceeded to Antwerp, safely detonating five magnetic mines, and the other seven cleared a channel from Breskens to Vlissingen, detonating nine ground mines. Captain Hopper estimated it would take 28 days to clear the whole way up to Antwerp, where the naval officer commanding agreed not to risk passing ships through before then.

Despite losing several working days to atrocious weather, Operation *Calendar* made good progress. Hopper nearly declared Antwerp safe on the 21st, but more mines were found next day, and sweeping continued. Finally, on 26 November, Antwerp was declared as safe as intensive minesweeping could make it. Twenty-two days after Operation *Calendar* began, and 85 after Antwerp had fallen into Allied hands, the first three coasters entered the docks, followed two days later by a convoy of Liberty ships. Total mines found in the river numbered 237 or 267, the most authoritative sources disagreeing. Two motor launches were blown up. Another 51 ground mines were found in the port, where clearing parties searched four million square yards of quayside. German night bombers and E-boats laid fresh mines in the river, but losses to these were few, and easily contained.

The opening of Antwerp as the principal supply port for the Allied armies in North-west Europe brought about a logistical revolution the strategic significance of which cannot be over stated. Paying tribute to First Canadian Army after the war, General Eisenhower thought the end of Nazism had been in clear view when the first ship moved unmolested up the Schelde. No longer would Allied forces suffer the supply bottlenecks that strangled their operations in the autumn of 1944. The cramped and shattered Channel ports became redundant, as was the Mulberry harbour at Arromanches, abandoned to the winter gales. In April 1945, the last full month of the North-west Europe campaign, Antwerp and its subsidiary facilities at Ghent handled 1.7 million tons, 60 per cent of all supplies landed in North-west Europe that month. Not only could the Allies nourish 84 divisions and their associated air squadrons, Antwerp's surplus capacity allowed them to feed Europe's liberated civilians and begin reconstruction of the shattered continent.

The Germans never had any doubt about Antwerp's importance, regarding it as a pistol pointed at the heart of the Reich. In December 1944, Hitler made it the ultimate objective of the Ardennes offensive. It also suffered the most sustained V-weapon offensive outside the British Isles. Before these attacks ended in March 1945, 1,214 V1 flying bombs and V2 ballistic missiles had fallen on the city, killing some 3,000 people, mostly civilians, and injuring 12,000 more. Two ships were sunk and 158 damaged, with little effect on use of the port, except that ammunition was rerouted via Ostend and Cherbourg.

For many, the liberation of Walcheren left a bitter taste. The Allies were not much further forwards than they had been in early September, before the Arnhem fiasco. Montgomery's refusal to give the Schelde the necessary priority ensured a dismal winter for the Dutch still in occupied Holland, and Allied troops on the sodden banks of the Maas. The opening of Antwerp came just in time. The first 10,000 tons of supplies cleared port a mere fortnight before the Ardennes offensive wrought havoc behind Allied lines. Masses of oil and petrol were destroyed. It was Antwerp that allowed the Allies to replace these, and weather the storm.

Walcheren itself was devastated; 87 per cent of its 47,000 acres (129,000ha) were left under water, with mines and booby traps everywhere. Even after the fighting was over, a naval shell rigged as a mine blew up one of 48 (RM) Commando's LVTs at Serooskerke. Twenty men died, including five of the crew, an officer and 13 men of the Royal Marines, and one medical orderly. The island's recovery was quicker than might have been expected, however. When 52nd Division moved out, its Royal Engineers stayed behind to restore essential services. 6 Cameronians spent a week in Vlissingen helping to clear the wreckage. Intelligence officers sought the German engineers responsible for laying the minefields, but they had departed in good time. Collaborators and POWs were pressed into service instead. A massive dyke repair exercise began, using Phoenix caissons left over from the Mulberry harbours. Most of the gaps were filled the October after their creation, the Rammekens Gap east of Vlissingen being finally closed in February 1946. Next year, the ground was sufficiently dry for new trees to be planted in place of those killed by the salt water. A new Walcheren had arisen, to replace the one that had been drowned as the price of Europe's freedom.

THE BATTLEFIELD TODAY

Walcheren is easily accessible, with numerous roads and cycle paths. The most startling difference from 1944 is the Sloe Channel's disappearance, making a peninsula. See Topografische kaart 'Middelburg 65 West', produced by Kadaster/Geo-Informatie, at 1:50,000, available in the UK. The E318 motorway links Walcheren to the mainland; hourly trains connect with international rail services at Roosendaal.

In Middelburg see the town hall and Daser's headquarters, five minutes away at 6 Damplein, opposite the bandstand. Hourly buses run to most parts of Walcheren from the railway station. Nearby, Middelburg Library houses numerous wartime images of Walcheren in the Zeeuwse Beeldbank, available online at www.zeeuwsebibliotheek.nl.

Vlissingen is an excellent base for a battlefield tour, with summer buses to Dishoek, Zoutelande, Westkapelle and Domburg. Most places of military interest lie along the seafront, from the Binnenhaven lock gates, past Uncle Beach (filled in) to the Oranjemolen, and a restored observation bunker open Sunday afternoons (May–November). See Bellamypark and monuments to 4th Commando Brigade and 155th Brigade in Commandoweg, on the site of Uncle Beach.

In Westkapelle there is an extensive view from the lighthouse, open Tuesdays, Thursdays and Sundays. Dutch victims of the bombing are buried nearby. Walcheren's British dead lie in the Commonwealth War Graves Commission cemetery at Bergen-op-Zoom. The Zuidstraat west of the tower has an SSEF memorial in the Markt church wall. The Polderhuis Museum is open daily (www.polderhuiswestkapelle.nl), while memorials to 4th Commando Brigade, 52nd Division and the SSEF are on the dyke behind Red Beach and on Green Beach.

The dunes between Westkapelle and Dishoek are accessible by footpaths along the top, cycle paths to landward or along the beach. Constant onshore winds blowing soft sand everywhere are a reminder of the commandos' difficulties.

Zoutelande on the Vlissingen–Westkapelle road has two restored bunkers in the dunes south of the church, open Wednesday and Sunday afternoons (May–November).

Stichting Bunkerbehoud maintains the bunker museums mentioned, contact at info@bunkerbehoud.com. Little remains of the batteries; W11 and W13 at Dishoek and Zuiderduin were in squares 025388 and 021392 of the modern 1:50,000 map; W15 and W17 lie beneath Westkapelle dyke and Domburg golf course, in squares 019395 and 022398.

FURTHER READING

Anon, *History of 47 (RM) Commando* RM Museum typescript, 1946

Anon, *The History of the 6th (Lanarkshire) Battalion the Cameronians (Scottish Rifles)* John Cossar: Glasgow, 1945

Anon, *The Story of 79th Armoured Division October 1942–June 1945* Hamburg, 1945

Blake, G., *Mountain and Flood: The History of the 52nd (Lowland) Division 1939–1946* Jackson & Son: Glasgow, 1950

BR 1736 (37) Admiralty Naval Staff Historical Section, Battle Summary No. 49 The Campaign in North West Europe June 1944–May 1945 HMSO: London, 1952

Chalmers, Rear Admiral W. S., *Full Circle: The Biography of Admiral Sir Bertram Ramsey* Hodder & Stoughton: London, 1959

Combined Operations Headquarters Bulletin Y/47, Combined Operations against Walcheren Island COHQ: London, 1945

Crucq, P. M., *Turning the Key: The Capture and Liberation of Walcheren October 30–November 8 1944* Private publication: Vlissingen 2009

Dear, I., *Ten Commando* Leo Cooper: Barnsley, 1987

Dunning, J., *The Fighting Fourth: No. 4 Commando at War 1940–45* Sutton: Stroud Gloucestershire, 1987

Ellis, Major L. F., *History of the Second World War: Victory in the West Vol II* HMSO: London, 1962

Forfar, J., *From Omaha to the Scheldt: The Story of 47 (RM) Commando* Tockwell Press: East Lothian, 2001

Ford, K., *D-Day Commando: From Normandy to the Maas with 48 Royal Marine Commando* Sutton: Stroud, 2003

Gunning, Captain H., *Borderers in Battle: the War Story of the King's Own Scottish Borderers* Berwick, 1948

Houterman, J. N., *Walcheren bevrijd* Private publication: Middelburg, 1994

Jackson, Colonel E. D., *War History of the 4th Battalion King's Own Scottish Borderers 1939–45* Galashiels, 1946

Linnell, T. G., *48 Royal Marine Commando, The Story* Private publication: 1946

McBain, Lieutenant-Colonel S. W., *A Regiment at War: The Royal Scots (The Royal Regiment) 1939–45* Pentland Press: Edinburgh, 1988

McDougall, M. C., *Swiftly They Struck: The Story of No. 4 Commando* Odhams: London, 1954

Mitchell, R., *They Did What Was Asked of Them: 41 (Royal Marines) Commando* Firebird Press: Poole, 1996

Moulton J. L., *Battle for Antwerp* Ian Allen: London, 1978

——, *Haste to the Battle* Cassell: London, 1963

Muir, A., *The First of Foot: The History of the Royal Scots (The Royal Regiment)* Royal Scots: Edinburgh, 1961

Naval Historical Branch, *The Alternative to Arnhem, Operation Infatuate, The Capture of Walcheren 1 November 1944 and the Opening of Antwerp* NHB: London, 1994

Philips, Colonel C. F. RM, *47 Cdo at Walcheren* RM Museum Archive, 7/19/3

Polderhuis Westkapelle, Dijk- en Oorlogsmuseum & Stichting Bunkerbehoud, *Memoria Walcheren 40–45: Een Oversicht van Oorlogsmonumenten en Restanten van de Atlantikwall* Polderhuis Museum: Westkapelle, 2007

Pugsley, Rear Admiral A. F., *Destroyer Man* Weidenfeld & Nicolson: London 1957

Rawling, G., *Cinderella Operation* Cassell: London 1980

Rawson, A., *Walcheren – Operation Infatuate* Leo Cooper: Barnsley 2003

Sakkers, H., *Vesting Vlissingen: Een veranderende vormgeving door de eeuwen heen* Stichting Bunkerbehoud: Middelburg, 2004

Shulman, M., *Defeat in the West* Secker & Warburg: London 1947 & 1968

Stacey, Colonel C. P., *The Canadian Army 1939–1945 An Official Historical Summary* Ministry of National Defence: Ottawa 1948

Thompson, R. W., *The Eighty Five Days: the Story of the Battle of the Scheldt* Hutchinson: London, 1957

Tullett, Captain E. V., *The Campaign in North West Europe: A History of the Fifth Battalion, the King's Own Scottish Borderers from 19 October 1944 until VE Day* Minden, 1945

Whitaker, W. D., and S., *The Battle of the Scheldt* Stoddart Publishing: Ontario, 1984

GLOSSARY

AGRA	Army Group Royal Artillery
AVRE	Armoured Vehicle Royal Engineers: Churchill tank with 12in. mortar
BMA	Beach Maintenance Area
Buffalo	see LVT
Flail	Sherman tank fitted to explode mines, alias Crab
FOB	Forward Observer Bombardment
FOO	Forward Observation Officer
FSU	Field Surgical Unit
HLI	Highland Light Infantry
KOSB	King's Own Scottish Borderers
LCA	Landing Craft Assault
LCG(L)	Landing Craft Gun (Large)
LCG(M)	Landing Craft Gun (Medium)
LCF	Landing Craft Flak
LCH	Landing Craft Headquarters
LCI(S)	Landing Craft Infantry (Small)
LCOCU	Landing Craft Obstacle Clearance Unit
LCP	Landing Craft Personnel
LCP(Sy)	Landing Craft Personnel (Survey)
LCS(L)	Landing Craft Support (Large)
LCT	Landing Craft Tank
LCT(R)	Landing Craft Tank (Rocket)
LVT	Landing Vehicle Tracked: amphibious personnel carrier or Buffalo
MAA	Marine-Artillerie-Abteilung (Naval Artillery Regiment)
MFA	Marine-Flak-Abteilung (Naval Anti-aircraft Regiment)
ML	Motor Launch
PIAT	Projectile Infantry Anti-tank
POW	Prisoner of War
RA	Royal Artillery
RCA	Royal Canadian Artillery
RCAMC	Royal Canadian Army Medical Corps
RE	Royal Engineers
RM	Royal Marines
SSEF	Support Squadron Eastern Flank
Vierling	Quadruple or four-barrelled
Weasel	Small unarmoured tracked amphibious personnel carrier

INDEX

Note: numbers in **bold** refer to illustrations and maps